One Track Minded:

How to Change Your Train of Thought

Katrina E. Johnson

I would like to dedicate this book to my children Taylor Johnson and Quentez Johnson for being the pivotal points in my life that ushered me into my varying stages of growth. The growth that I experienced has sharpened and fostered my passion to write and eventually create a manual that intends to light the path of anyone struggling to find the switch.

Acknowledgments

I cannot express enough thanks to Shunta Murray, one of my dearest friends. She provided motivation and loaned her ears for many suggestions and her eyes for many drafts of my book prior to its completion. I offer my sincerest appreciation for the title, "School Teacher," she adorned me with because while teaching is not my current profession, I have always made myself available to those eager to grow on any level and in varying directions, just as a teacher does.

My completion of this project could not have been accomplished without the support of my family and children. To you all, thank you for allowing me to wear many hats throughout our growth as a unit and during our individual victories. Special thanks to my parents, Brenda Johnson and Ernest Johnson (deceased) for seeing my potential early in life and doing whatever they could to foster any activity that propelled my passion. I am especially thankful for the first typewriter I received for Christmas in 5th Grade, no more dolls.

Finally, to my caring, loving, and supportive younger self. Your encouragement when the times got rough are much appreciated and noted. It was a great comfort and relief to know that you were willing to take a bullet, step on a grenade, and fall on your sword to ensure that I got to where I am now, paving the way to getting to where I'm supposed to be. My heartfelt thanks.

Contents

INTRODUCTION

"To put the world in order, we must first put the nation in order; to put the nation in order, we must first put the family in order; to put the family in order; we must first cultivate our personal life; we must first set our hearts right." **Confucius**

Confucius' quote is intriguing in its simplicity; it points out the importance of change and its vessel-like nature as it carves the path towards growth. Despite the quote being dated, its relevance in society today is substantial. I haven't studied society to ensure that my allegation is correct, however, I am sharing my experience with change and the benefits that outweigh the pain. I do not claim to be an anthropologist or have a profound knowledge of the actions or inaction of people, however, my years of experience in the silent study of people has provided me with a different lens. With an enlightened mindset and vision, I aim to provide a bit of foresight to those who opt for change, no matter the pain.

When I set out to write this book, it took me a while, about 8 years a while. I had so many of what I thought were random, sorted ideas. They were sorted in the sense that they would come to me in streams of consciousness at the most random times. I would wake up in the middle of the night to write something on my phone's notepad or jot down notes or phrases that came to me in my dreams. While it looked like gibberish, it made sense in the weird way that my mind processes things.

After tying everything together, I decided that what I had was an opportunity to bring the same energy to my life that I would to a good recipe. Just like with a good recipe, if you add the right seasonings, it will be amazing, and everyone will want it. With recipes, you follow the instructions until you feel led to make decisions that better fit your desired taste. If you take the boxed version of any dish, you can tailor it to meet your needs; it's the same thing when figuring out life. You are led to lead, even if you're the only one following.

In a world filled with constant change and uncertainties, finding solace within us becomes paramount. It is in moments of doubt and despair that faith emerges as a guiding light, illuminating our paths and empowering us to navigate the complexities of life. This faith-based self-help book serves as a beacon of hope, reminding us that within each of us lies an incredible reservoir of strength, resilience, and untapped potential.

Drawing from personal wisdom from various spiritual encounters and personal anecdotes of triumph over adversity, this book unveils the transformative power of faith as a catalyst for self-discovery and personal growth. Through its pages, you will embark on a journey uncovering the depths of your aspirations. Creating an opportunity to take the first step in the reorganization of your reality is a challenge worth pursuing and a journey worth taking.

Discover how change can empower you to embrace your faith, conquer fear, and overcome limiting beliefs. Explore the process of surrendering to a higher power, allowing divine guidance to shape your life's course. Learn to cultivate change, gratitude, resilience, and compassion, nourishing your soul and fostering harmonious relationships with others.

Guided by personal insights, you will embark on a transformative passage to change through the institution of prayer and meditation. With faith as your steadfast companion, you will be equipped with the tools needed to awaken new potential, transcending the obstacles that hinder your personal growth and fulfillment.

Through the transformative power of faith, embark on a journey toward self-discovery and spiritual awakening. Let this book serve as a roadmap, illuminating the path to unlocking your innate abilities and unleashing the boundless possibilities that lie within you. Together, let us start a remarkable voyage of faith, harnessing its profound wisdom to cultivate a life filled with purpose, joy, and an unwavering belief in our limitless potential.

In the chapters ahead, we will undertake a journey of change, newfound knowledge, and fostering resilience through faith. By accepting the insight shared, we can nurture our inner strength, deepen our trust in a higher power, and emerge from life's trials with renewed resilience and unwavering faith. Life is an ever-changing journey filled with both moments of joy and seasons of hardship. Through personal anecdotes and insight, we discover that even in the darkest storms, faith can be our guiding light, illuminating the path to change, personal growth, healing, and, ultimately, a life filled with peace.

Chapter One
CHOICES

Am I the only one guilty of procrastination?

To solve a problem, you must acknowledge that it exists. This is me admitting that I had a problem with procrastination. Upon investigating the root cause of this plague, comfort was found to be the culprit. Never in a million years did I expect that one of the few things that brought me joy and comfort is not a gift but also a curse.

I don't know about you, but I was devastated by this revelation. This was as traumatic as my childhood discovery that stepping on a crack did not break my mother's back and unmasking the truth that Friday the 13th is not unlucky, it's my lucky day. I'm also guilty of getting off on a tangent, but that's a whole other thing. Imagine something you have been attempting to obtain for years being the one reason you have become stagnant. Imagine subconsciously deciding where your success will stop because you're COMFORTABLE!

Once the shock subsided, I had to find a rational starting point. I wanted to ensure that I didn't venture too far back in thought because it's super easy to get lost in the past, especially the good parts. Strolling through the old memory bank, I found the exact moment I decided I was comfortable. It was about a year ago. I was making great money at a new job with a phenomenal bonus structure, in love with my new home, and enjoying a new car; I mean, things were clicking on all cylinders. I was comfortable...or so I thought.

In revisiting that moment, it was the routine and the order that was so alluring and attractive. My desire to control and not flow were inevitably a part of the problem The illusion of control was captivating, addictive, a beautiful lie. I was mesmerized; everything had a place, and everyone was neatly compartmented. Yep, life was good. Despite my believing this was my desired objective, the look of it made me uneasy; I had an underlying desire for a bit of chaos, organized, of course.

My unsettling realization is I no longer desire

comfort since it has become detrimental to my growth and success. I have decided to abandon my comfort to introduce a bit of disorder because change does not happen in comfort or order. Change is inevitable and necessary for continued growth. Who would dare to abandon the opportunity for change to wallow in the contentment of comfort? I would rather choose to be the change I want to see. I made my choice that day.

Choices are decisions before they mature. Choices are free-spirited, easy-going, fancy-free, without a care in the world because they've got plenty of options. Decisions, on the other hand, are more uptight. Decisions get that they wasted a lot of options when they were choices and very likely sought the opinion of too many people, who had been haunted by their own choices, and were now difficult to take; no one wants to end up with a difficult decision.

There are two types of choices and two types of decisions: hard and difficult. If you make the hard choice, you'll have more tests, but you'll learn more lessons in a shorter amount of time, specifically if you pass the test the first time around. By passing the tests, you put yourself in a position where your decisions are easy because you opted for experience. On the other hand, if you choose to make all the easy choices, you'll end up with difficult decisions because you've kicked so much down the road. You've got to the bridge, and it's now time to cross it. In a nutshell, if you put off what you could do today for tomorrow, you may either never get the opportunity or you may not have the time. Time is borrowed, not promised.

What Is Change?

Change is defined by the Oxford English Dictionary as "the act or instance of making or becoming different." This definition rings true; I'm abandoning comfort for something to become something different, the truest sentiment ever uttered. If change were an acronym, it would equate to the notion that CHOOSING HOW ACCOUNTABILITY NAVIGATES GOOD ENERGY.

Choosing change requires devising a plan that will bring about a new look, feel, or experience, whichever is being sought. Maybe it's just a collective change; only time will tell, and divine timing will dictate. I'm a firm believer that our desire for change, if truly desired, arises from our preparation for the inevitable. By deciding to prepare or plan, you are allotted an opportunity to introduce faith into the scenario. Faith is our silent partner. It isn't something tangible, but you allow it to serve as your support system. You allow faith to "stand in the gap," so to speak.

Faith is traditionally tied to a higher power, an energy or power greater than yourself that aids in the process of change by providing guidance or an ordering of your steps once you get the plan together. Now, there are instances when you may feel like your faith isn't enough and maybe you've had some missteps, or worse, you've lost your footing on the path. Any confusion you feel is a distraction. Even if you have gotten off the path, the last thing you want to do is to take time to engage in something negative like beating yourself up; nope, that would be the true distraction.

The illusion I had chosen had grown unsettling. The comfort has forced me into an overthinking spiral that was disrupting my mental health. Of course, I decided that this unsettled feeling of lack of comfortability was a call to action, and like a lot of people, I acted. I decided to quit my job because, yep, that was the solution, WRONG! I still felt antsy. I had to do something else. I admit quitting my job was indeed liberating, frightening, and confusing, but I didn't feel like my actions were totally off the mark. The next thing I did was move into a smaller place because it was just me. I had a 4-bedroom home for only me. I downsized to a 2-bedroom townhome; yes, two bedrooms. I need my "thinking space." LOL!

Change comes with persistence and trials. We must test different ways of doing things to know what will and won't work. It is in the introduction of the options and opportunities that we truly figure out how change arises and becomes consistent, which is the objective. During the process of changing, some things will feel comfortable, confusing, weird, unnerving, satisfying, sad, and a bit emotional. The myriad of emotions you may experience are a part of the process. Allowing yourself to feel the emotions in the present moment in which it is occurring allows you to process what has happened through the feelings only relative to that moment.

For example, in forming anything there is a stirring. Whether you are stirring eggs for breakfast, cement for the foundation of a building, or mixing two paints to form one, there is a "controlled" disruption that gets you the desired eggs, foundation, and paint match. During the process of change, we struggle with old ways, old responses, and old emotions because they are comfortable and our immediate desired reaction in familiar situations.

There is a saying that "when we know better, we do better." This is a phenomenal statement and quite inspirational, save for the fact that people are creatures of habit, and old habits die hard. The desire to change will overcome the comfort of old habits. The change will trigger pushback from others, but that's not your problem. When instances arise where your goals conflict with someone else's agenda, you're the priority; this is not an instance of compromise.

The Process of Change

The process of change itself requires a few things. Firstly, you choose to change. Anything we are forced into prematurely, on someone else's timeline, back-sliding is imminent. Next, we must honor change. As weird as it sounds, things we do not give honor to, we tend to devalue, disregard, and dismiss. When honor is introduced, there is a level of respect that is bestowed upon the person, place, thing, or task that is being embarked upon. The acceptance of change and its process is imperative in the uphill battle that is changing. There is a point in the process where you are no longer in the proverbial curve and the stride feels natural.

Because the change is new, we must nurture it. Nurturing change requires us to forgive ourselves for missteps and allow for the correction of mistakes. By forgiving ourselves, it gets easier to forgive others. By forgiving others with more ease, it can comestimes lay the foundation for instances where we get pushback from others. While we cannot control the actions of others, we can control our response to their behaviors or actions. We foster the success of our change by nurturing the new change and growth by not coddling it but by meeting the challenge head-on and combating old ways with change.

We must grant change the space to exist within us, expand into the environment around us, and evoke it when the opportunity presents itself. It is a phenomenal thing that allows for the fulfillment of our expectations. It is a vessel that allows us to envision possibilities as we demolish obstacles, self-imposed and otherwise. It is every opportunity that we encounter daily. Lastly, after granting change the space to elevate you, encouraging change is a must.

By choosing change, you have decided that there is a desirable situation or circumstance that exists in your reality and instead of electing one of the most popular go-tos, complaining, you have opted to take the first step to be the change you want to see. It is easier to take a more pedestrian role in your life, especially when you are satisfied with some, most, or all aspects of it. My question is, if you decide to become a voyeur in your own life or elect to ride along in your life as a passenger, who is there to blame or complain to at the curtain call? We all have aspects of our lives that we would like to see differently whether it be a revived love life, a more financially rewarding career, or a better home. Some instances are a call to action, but then there are scenarios to be still and allow things to unfold. The objective is to use our discernment to determine the difference between "go time" and "chill time."

Discernment

Discernment is described as "the ability to judge well" or "the perception in the absence of judgment to obtain spiritual guidance and understanding." Discernment is an intricate part of the ushering in of the application and the consistency of change. It is relevant in the sense that it works as a compass, directing you in the right way in which you should go. The compass with the magnetic needle guides us in travels of the world just as our discernment through the voice, wisdom, and guidance of God leads us through life's twists and turns, knowns and unknowns.

Challenge yourself to be a spiritual being having a human experience. Allow yourself to get into the flow of life and be led to the inevitable path of change. Flow unknowingly with the energy of your higher power. You are moving in silence and not announcing intentions, private missteps, or casually resetting while reconnecting with your path. There is no one to acknowledge the mistake; as unfortunate as it is, not everyone is rooting for you. Believe yourself to be the person you aspire to be and act as if you are already that person by carrying yourself as such. Dress for the job you want, not the job you have.

Constraints are physical and limits are mental. We can succeed at any task we set our minds to. It is our mindset that carries the seeds of our thoughts, our words that foster the change, and our actions that cultivate the change into fruition. It is through our thoughts, words, and actions that change is given the opportunity to spread its wings and grow. Our thoughts are seeds formed by what we take in with our senses. Depending on our energy during the time of conception, the thought will either be birthed as positive or negative. The nature of our thoughts determines the taste of our words; they will either be sweet, bitter, salty, sharp, etc. Our actions will present themselves as either offensive, defensive, or neutral. When we realize we must be a part of the creation of our reality and not solely rely upon the higher power, god, or supreme being to write the script and operate us as puppets, free will is our right, our choice, and the expectation imposed upon us. We are not tied or bound in any particular situation because anything that we choose to not change is a choice.

Once the choice is made to pursue change, to be successful, you must avoid the exits, sacrifice and compromise. While it is easy to become distracted at any exit on the road to successful change, you must stay in the lane of consistency to avoid the slow of comfort, procrastination, and cravings to compare your position in your journey to that of another. Making the choice to change will prove challenging as you are allowed a chance to prioritize yourself on the road to attaining what will solidify or affirm your happiness. In indulging in self-awareness that leads to self-actualization, we are discarding the opinions of others and prioritizing what we intend to tackle first to ensure we achieve self-fulfillment.

There are no two people purposed with the same journey, meaning there are no two people with the same destination, hence, solidifying the notion that we are running our own race and we are our own competition. Imagine how many people are fearful of the notion that they are the reason they are not as successful as they feel they should be at any given point in their lives.

Faith

Have you ever felt all alone, like you were all you had, like you couldn't count on anyone, and ended up having a day where everything that could go wrong did, a real Murphy's Law type day for the records? What do you do in those instances? How do you respond to what equates to being a day that drives you to the point of wanting to throw in the towel? I think we've all been there, but how do you handle that type of day? Do you blow your top? Do you allow yourself to just lose it, releasing the venomous amount of negativity and dissatisfaction onto some unsuspecting individual, hence spreading agitation and frustration into an already impatient, volatile circumstance? My response to all of this...enter the faith stage.

Faith, to me, is the process of **Forgetting About It To Heal**. Perhaps it's not that simple, but isn't it? There are definitions of faith but why seek to define it when you would much rather feel it, experience it, carry it, wear it, revel in it, or take solace in it. It is ludicrous to think of someone attempting to garner, distribute, oversee, dismantle, remove, diminish, or abolish the faith of another. How arrogant is the individual who attempts to rob someone of their faith or dilute their faith or practices of faith due to a disagreement of views or disbelief of what another holds dear and sacred?

Forgiveness is the first thing that comes to mind when I consider faith. We must first forgive ourselves in any situation where there is unrest or disruption, as that is the first step towards change. There is no harm in a disagreement as long as it remains civil. In attempting to persuade another in any respect, we must respect the opinion despite disagreeing. Nature and nurture have shaped the thoughts of every individual, and contrary to popular belief, more times than not, an individual is always willing to debate their truth, which should be allowed peacefully. When we forgive ourselves, it is easier to forgive others. Forgiveness is intricate to change on any level.

Acceptance is key in change because differences must be acknowledged on the road to common ground. While common ground is the objective, depending on the nature of the change, this may be like pulling teeth. As I said, people love to debate their truth, fact-based or experience-rooted. It may take multiple conversations for the emergence or appearance of change, but there is no platform for change without accepting that differences are ever evident and prevalent and need only be addressed and given the room to breathe.

Initiation is a word that comes to mind when thinking about faith and change. You must open the door for change by expressing the desire for its commencement and the choice to embark upon its path. By taking the steps necessary to usher in a new ideal littered with possibilities and opportunities, you are carving the road less taken in pursuit of the unknown. When you speak of change, faith is called to action as the lubricant that greases the wheels of consistency.

Trusting the process is the most important aspect of change. It is easy to attempt to measure our growth by that of others, but that is the weirdest thing ever. That's as crazy as having a different diet, body type, body shape, metabolism and other contributing factors, and then wondering why you do not weigh the same. There are no two spirits with the same purpose and destiny. Our lives are a culmination of our choices and our decisions, not mirroring the life of someone because of how it appears on the outside. We must make a concerted effort to learn to trust the unknown and to take solace in not knowing. We go to bed every night and make plans for tomorrow because there is an expectation that we will have an opportunity to follow through with the plans we set forth. How naive are we to negate the fact that time is desired but not guaranteed?

Two of the worst things you will ever encounter are negativity and expectations. The sad part about the two worst things is that people choose to carry them wherever they go. It's odd to think that a person walks into a room with a negative attitude and negative energy and wonders why they are not well received. You receive what you project. If you don't like what you're receiving, change the mirror image you're projecting, and you become the change you want to see. When it comes to expectations, it baffles me that people arrive in any situation with the mental notion of what will be; that is a bit presumptuous, to say the least. You are responsible for your expectations if you bring them to any situation. Any attempt to assert or impose your expectations on another is a fast track to disappointment. There should be no attempt to force or browbeat a person into what you want; it's selfish, unfair, manipulative and, yep, low vibrational. The attempt at emotional manipulation is a negative action that breeds discomfort, dissension, and distrust, which should be disappointing.

Healing is at the root of faith and the center of change. Wounds are the result of the pain that pushes you to change. They must heal for the change to commence. There must be a concerted effort to forgive the ones that caused the hurt, accept the flaws of others, initiate the actions that foster the change, trust that the process is palpable, and head towards healing. When an offense occurs that causes an emotional injury, the healing begins when we decide to stop retelling the story. Repetitively telling the story is reopening the wound, pulling off the scab and poking it, allowing someone else to weigh in on the matter, and extending the healing process. Often people are so distracted by the inconvenience brought on by the negative happening that they do not realize that what is happening is an opportunity to give grace and to move on.

When simplified, change is choosing how accountability navigates good energy. Positive energy and outlook are important when establishing the consistency that serves as the vessel that propels change. Accepting the necessity of change is intricate to the success of the process of change itself. While it is easy to get comfortable with the mundane within the day-to-day, change is ever present and necessary for the growth of the societal collective. Change, while occasionally fear provoking, must acknowledge that fear is merely false energy appearing real.

Change is the exit that must be taken on the road to success. It makes way for healing and eventual growth. By choosing the path of change, following a situation that may be emotionally damaging or scarring, we fast-track the process to healing. Upon accepting the offense of another, you have decided to move on from the circumstance by forgiving or giving grace to yourself as the victim while extending the same to the offender. While the adjustment of giving grace may change how you are, the objective is to not change who you are.

Chapter Two

HEALING

"Sticks and stones may break my bones, but words shall never hurt me" is a nursery rhyme once recited by children, likely at the behest of their parents or teachers. This nursery rhyme was likely created to deter children from teasing one another or making fun of each other. Despite knowing that words, in fact, can and do hurt if used in a rude, mean, or derogatory manner, adults perpetuated the lie in the name of "saving children" from their harsh peers. While it's interesting to assume that the choice was made to shield children from the truth, it reads more like deception.

To put off something for tomorrow that could be done today is the American way. The notion of kicking things down the road only leaves a larger pile to gather and sort at the end of the day. If words are indeed harmless, as the nursery rhyme implies, are therapists, psychiatrists, and psychologists scam artists? Is mental health a worldwide conspiracy with no legs and a bunch of malarkey? Childhood trauma is a real thing, and countless adults are living proof that words do hurt and can cause wounds that take years to heal, but there's always HOPE.

What happens to a sore or wound that you pick and poke? The wound will become infected and spread, causing further injury. For emotional wounds to heal, you must first admit that you were, at some point, wronged. No one wants to be seen as a victim because society paints victims as weak, feeble, and unable to take care of themselves. As unfortunate as that sounds, those same generalizations make people prone to victimization. When it comes to words, the intention of the speaker, aggressor, agitator, or instigator has one sole purpose, and that is to get you out of your peace and off of your proverbial "sweet spot." We've all heard misery loves company; this rings truer than you know.

The trajectory of our reality is manufactured in the collaboration of our thoughts, words, and actions. The root of our words, thoughts, and actions are in our intentions. Our intentions are molded by what is perceived and processed by our five senses, which subsequently form our reality. Our senses operating in unison form the foundation of our reality, while it is our engagement with others that develop the rich tapestry of our layers. We choose our positive or negative reality by choosing or deciding if we will be one that life is happening to or one life is happening for. It is the difference between a life of inconveniences and a life of opportunities. It is your perception that sets the stage for your Broadway headlining show called life. Our hope is found in our goals, dreams, and desires. It is written that where there is no vision, the people will perish.

Hope is commandeered via our thoughts of optimism, the employment of optimistic words, and the introductive display of purposeful, intention-laden actions. When speaking to ourselves, it should be personalized training on how to treat others. It is in engagement with others that we are prompted with the opportunity and task to teach others how to treat us. In teaching others how to treat us, we are providing a blueprint to others that conveys what is and what is not acceptable or what will or will not be received. Words are intricate in the "teaching" period after meeting people because, with people, we must stand on business when it comes to our emotional, mental, and physical well-being.

People are creatures of habit, and it becomes automatic to group people together out of comfort or laziness, depending on who you ask. It is quite lazy to impose your judgment on an individual and justify your treatment of a person just because of "your" preconceived notions and ability to "judge a book by its cover." How pleasurable it must be to cast a person aside due to narrow-minded views, which you're entitled to. When the generalizations emerge, the comfort of using particular words and phrases comes into play. As the attitude of "I know your kind" rears its ugly head, it is in these instances that thoughts are shared, words are spewed, and actions are displayed; this is where emotional wounds are born.

In situations where others choose to be hypercritical or judgmental, we must take steps to preserve our hope. We must offer grace to those ill-advised, unlearned, ignorant, spiteful, or just hurt because hurt people, hurt people. By giving grace first to ourselves, we can heal the wounds that cannot be covered by bandages. With grace, we are exchanging trauma, drama, and turmoil for peace. In our choice to not walk the road of those before us or by opting to be the change you want to see, we reestablish hope and reset the path to a positive narrative. Giving others grace takes practice and motivation, much like exercise; you know it'll pay off in the long run, it just takes some getting used to. With time, consistency, and faith, giving grace to others, despite their shortcomings, is essential because it's less to unpack in any new situation, environment, or relationship. We must lead by change, no matter how intimidating, frightening, or unsettling. Pursuing the unknown is paramount to growth.

Have you ever been in a situation where you didn't know what the outcome would be, but you were too afraid to trust the unknown? Can you think of a time or an instance where all odds say that you should lose or things won't go your way, but then it all falls into place for your benefit? Do you recall a time when you gave what you didn't have and, in turn, you walked into more than you gave away, but you wondered how it was possible? I can answer yes to each one of these questions.

When you are in the business of feeling like you

are all you have, you can't count on anyone, and nothing good or positive will ever happen for you, you have chosen a path of negativity that will only generate and breed negative thoughts, feelings, and actions. If you choose a road of negativity, there is no place for positive thoughts, actions, feelings, or responses because we receive what we project. Once a house of negativity has been built with your words, there is no room for positivity until you "clean house." By cleaning house, you hit your personal reset button, allowing your new feelings to transform your new thoughts, introducing more positive, satisfying actions that change what you project as you have new inhabitants, more positive inhabitants.

I will admit that there was a time when I was in the business of always expecting the worst but not really preparing for the best. I didn't appear openly negative, but I did a great job of standing in my own way and missing out on opportunities to meet the right people, subsequently removing me from the proverbial "right place, right time" situation. It wasn't until someone pointed it out to me that the words I used did a great job of dousing my dreams and desires before they could even take form. This same person enlightened me on the power of our words and that despite the old mantra we were all taught as children, "sticks and stones may break my bones, but words will never hurt me," was the farthest thing from the truth. We must unlearn the notion that words are not powerful and accept that we give them power with the context and their introduction into any circumstance or conversation.

A positive mind is a peaceful and productive mind. Whether it's believed or perceived as fact or fiction, the heart is our mind's eye. It is our feelings and not our thoughts that reign truest. Our hearts are the generators from which our most honest feelings vibrate and circulate. To speak in statements such as "I feel" as opposed to "I think" expresses that you have gone internally to consider the situation, enlisted the candor of your heart and intuition, and surmised a subjective response, lacking the conjecture from "field agents" also known as the outside world. When responding with "I think" as a counter to an inquiry, the respondent provides a reply that is objective in style and encompasses an individual's past experience, stories from others, and any exposure ingested by our sensory notification system.

In engaging with others, it is most beneficial to us to speak from a place of honesty and purity, from our heart.

Our perception of what we take in with our ears and eyes strongly impacts what formulates in our minds, triggers our thoughts, and subsequently influences our reality. Whether it be through TV, radio, or our engagement with others, our thoughts, be they positive or negative, can be transformed into something other than what we intend. Our visual perceptions and auditory hallucinations can pit us against our own mental well-being. It's equivalent to having an orator narrate your life and they refuse to read what is written or report things as they are; it's like their sole purpose and agenda is to ensure that you lose. Does it sound far-fetched that it is our own actions and reactions can be shaped and molded to create a narrative alternate to the one we desire? By introducing a method called pausitivity into your day-to-day life, you can put yourself in a position where you teach yourself to speak constant positive results into your life by being the conductor of your train of thoughts.

Pausitivity

What is pausitivity? Pausitivity is the ability to train your mind to stop a negative thought on its track by counteracting it with a positive thought, redirecting the train of thought completely. It is through pausitivity that we can reset a train of thought to maintain a positive mindset. In fact, pausitivity would be the equivalent of opening an umbrella to avoid the wetness from the rain. In a situation where a negative thought should arise, you would simply immediately introduce a positive thought or multiple positive thoughts to counteract the negative thought, hence, taking control of a situation that could go negative or go off the rails.

I wouldn't go as far as to make a guarantee in the likelihood of success. However, in the pursuit of anything we desire, we throw caution to the wind. We are unmoved by the naysayers and deaf to the pessimists, left with our own voice and thoughts. It is in the moments where we take charge that, at times, our fears are the loudest, attempting to weaken the foundation. It is through practice and persistence of pausitivity that we allow ourselves an opportunity to reach our dreams and achieve our desires.

By using our own words and actions to write the stories of our lives, the thoughts and opinions of others are merely commentary. Just as movies have critics, so does our reality. The opinions of others are just that, the opinions of others. If you allow the observation of someone else to dilute the purity of your passion or if you allow someone else's fear of your success to supersede your destiny, you have relinquished the power necessary to obtain your dreams.

We feed into what we become with our thoughts, our words, and our actions. To think positively is to act positively. If positivity is what is within you, then positivity is what is projected. This is the equivalent of squeezing an orange and getting orange juice. Whether you agree with this or not, it makes sense to be able to successfully project any emotion you intend through controlling your intake, hence, controlling output.

Negative self-talk is an emotional prison. Since words build the houses we live in, speaking uplifting, optimistic, goal-oriented words and phrases to ourselves is us planting seeds of success. Once our mind hears that intention set, it goes to work on the positive actions we have initiated with our thoughts and words. When you have affirming thoughts that convert into favorable, motivating words, pour them into others, resonating and generating good energy in the universe.

We must abandon old ways of thinking and deconstruct old paradigms. Words are nothing more than a grouping of letters and sounds that we give meaning to. It is through our manipulation, application, and introduction of varying words and phrases that the scripts of our lives are written. It is through trial and error, living, that we gain the understanding that we are in charge of both the actions and reactions in our reality, and it is then that we understand our roles as producer, director, and star in this stage play we call life. Just as an artist creates works of art, so do we create our own reality, be it positive or negative.

Paradigms

In the instant negativity comes knocking, you must allow faith to answer the door. Once negativity enters the home of your spirit, like unwanted guests, it finds a comfortable place and resides until being thrown out or told to leave. When negativity becomes your roommate, there is no room for positivity because unless you stop it at the door, it will get comfortable and quickly fill your body, ruining your home and place of peace and solace. Negativity spreads like a virus, like a pandemic; positivity extinguishes negativity. Believe it or not, one thought is what needs to be introduced to get you on the road to recovery. I'd like to think that thought replacement therapy is key to "cleaning your house."

We are born with free will. As children, we are permitted to have fun, explore, be silly, and dream. In some instances, in our youths, we engage in entrepreneurial ventures by way of lemonade stands or school fundraisers, imbedding the desire to work within one's own defined parameters. Where does that passion go as we go from babes to youths to productive members of society coexisting in the Matrix? Due to societal norms, our parents, at some point, steer us towards something different but the same, just as they were reared and programmed. We are ushered away from our individuality and desires to be different to avoid ridicule and being singled out, herded towards something "safe."

College is always emphasized as "the" option after high school, not "an" option. We are programmed to follow the path of going to college, selecting a career, marrying, having children, and reinstalling the program. If ever there was a time to abandon the old paradigms, this is it. Going against the traditional blueprint and embarking upon the road less taken requires casting caution to the wind and allowing yourself to be led as opposed to the illusion of control. Seeing things as they are and making changes accordingly in pursuit of your dreams is one of the most satisfying things in the world...scary but necessary.

At some point, it was decided that creativity is a bad thing, free-thinking became frowned upon, and individuality was scoffed at. Society is enamored with the repetition and duplication of things that once were, calling them "re-boots" or "revamping." Why must we continue to consume the regurgitation of others to obtain someone else's version of normalcy? Those afraid of uniqueness, aspirational entrepreneurial spirits, and innovative creatives will stifle any idea that warrants ripples and threatens to dismantle the model where everything and everyone has a place.

When was the election held where the ballots were cast, and through a landslide, we lost our right to choose what we become, who we become, and when we become? When did we choose to become someone other than who we are, abandoning our destiny to be an indoctrinated, duplicated, reproduced droid? Are you currently walking the course meant for you? Are the shoes you're wearing your size crafted to fit only you and that you fancy so much that every day you rise, you can't wait to slide them back on? If you desire to become the director of the Broadway show called "My Life," turn the page and take the first step in writing the script for the rest of your life... cast with caution.

Just as a lawyer practices law or a doctor practices medicine, we must understand that the routine of practicing faith will become a habit that is second nature. To get into the practice of getting out of your own way, you must take the first step of forgiving yourself for all past transgressions and allow yourself a clean slate. Stop accepting that you are your own worst enemy or your biggest critic; this is not something to be proud of. When forgiving yourself, you choose to give more attention to your responses in any given situation to ensure that you take a beat, taking the time to present the version of yourself you're reestablishing for your personal well-being and mental health.

With complaining being one of the easiest jobs in the world, permit yourself to be led by your intuition, choosing the inspiration of change, and withdrawing from the frustration of continued harmful, hurtful behavior and projections. By deciding to change or redirect your thoughts, you reinstitute the trust you once had in your mind. You accept the truth that you conduct your train of thought despite any trials. By allowing yourself to remain transparent, you alleviate the anxiety that can possibly trigger the negative thoughts that can trigger a snowball of pessimistic thoughts, words, or actions. To choose to halt the negative runaway train of thought is to accept the start of the healing process that is necessary for the rewiring geared towards a constant positive mindset and eventually walking in your true purpose.

You can't sell it until you buy it. In short order, this means that once change happens in your life, true change, you won't feel obligated to announce it or try to convince people of it, or sell it. Change is felt; it shows it's seen, and it doesn't have to be highlighted. If a person has chosen change of their own volition, the process is private, making all successes and failures yours and yours alone

When you choose to keep your actions private, you allow yourself the opportunity to fail or succeed without an audience, opinions, judgment, and the weight of someone else's expectations or ridicule. People cannot measure what they did not grow, meaning you should not allow someone to judge you or your process because they don't know where you are or where you're going. This is the equivalent of someone watching a movie from the middle and trying to explain the plot; it's half the story. Paradigm shifts are our saving grace in our pursuit of change.

Healing is a step in the process of change. While it seems unrelated, accepting what has happened is vital in moving forward toward the things that will happen or are happening. Choosing to be distracted by things that, once they have occurred, are in our rearview will put us in a position where we will miss the exit to our destiny. Healing gives us an opportunity to figure out how we possibly contributed to the offense. By holding ourselves accountable for any role we may have had in the matter, we have opened the door for change to exist. When we choose to foster more positive thoughts, words, and actions, we allow room for change to thrive on the journey to growth.

By deciding to plant the seed of change, we are sowing a plant that will take time and effort to expand. The timing schedule will be divine, so we must always be aligned with patience because change is a process that will not be rushed lest reverting to old habits will arise. People are creatures of habit and old habits die hard; it is easy to abandon the train of change for a familiar track. If you're not a hamster or gerbil, it is wise to opt out of living your life on the wheel that spins but is going nowhere. To avoid regret, open the door to change; it's knocking.

Healing and change are not for the weak, but with practice, much like a muscle, the ability to do both is strengthened. Taking the approach of dedication to growth, we gain tenacity and courage that serve as allies along the process. True healing is a transformative process that demands honesty and vulnerability. By confronting our darkest fears and insecurities, we choose to rewrite our own narratives. Change is an inside job that requires us to break free from limiting beliefs and old patterns that no longer serve us. We must be willing to step outside of our comfort zone to embrace discomfort as a necessary part of growth. Healing and change are not easy, but they are worth it. They allow us to shed the layers of pain and fear that hold us back from becoming the best versions of ourselves. So be bold in your pursuit of healing and change because you deserve nothing less than to evolve into the person you were born to be and not the one you were told you were.

Chapter Three

ACCOUNTABILITY

The Court of Accountability

While engaging with people, I found more people are willing to place blame as opposed to accepting it. I have heard tons of arguments where no one started, everyone took part in it, someone decided to keep it going, and no one ended it. It never ceases to amaze me that people will go back and forth about the most trivial things to the extent that friendships are ended, relationships are damaged, and discourse is certain. Imagine being so hungry for the last word that you starve the one person who you feel understood you. Think about how many times you chose to be right over keeping, maintaining, or introducing peace.

I always make a concerted effort not to argue one's truth because once the commitment is established, that is not a marriage easily dissolved. However, I will hold anyone accountable for intended discourse or melee. I have little to no concern about having the last word or correcting one that does not want to be corrected; my goal is always to grow and enlighten. With my intention of aiding anyone who desires to move forward with a view that is broad and layered, I hold the court of accountability daily to ensure that I am successful at being a better version of myself every day.

Imagine there was a court that you had to go to for moral violations. A court where accountability is enforced in a way that you get to see the long-term consequences of your moral offenses. I would say that's the job of the conscience, but someone is either lying down on the job or has just abandoned their post and gone AWOL. With the dismissive nature people take today when it comes to "owning their shit," throwing rocks and hiding your hands seems to be a going trend.

As thoughts remain unseen and unread, we are responsible for the words we speak and the actions we display. Passing the buck and finger-pointing are a couple of ways I've seen people dodge accountability, like an inmate dodges a shank in a prison fight. Just as everyone has the right to bear arms, we have the right to free speech. Every word that comes out of our mouth costs something, and you'll pay one way or the other unless you decide to run it through upstairs (in your head) before bringing it downstairs for presentation (out of your mouth). While it's easy to speak casually and cavalierly with the expectation of no recourse, you must not allow your mouth to write any checks that you are unable to cash. Many speak as if they are Rhodes' scholars and mouths of prayer books. Delusion is more than a noun; it's a virus that is spreading rampantly in society.

Accountability would provide the opportunity to review things from a point of view where you ask yourself, was I actively listening or waiting to respond and express my feelings? Did I give them an opportunity to express their feelings? Why did I get so angry? Was there truth in their accusation? While the questions asked may vary depending on the issue at hand, I purposely referenced "I" questions to express that in any given situation, we can only control our actions, reactions, thoughts, and feelings. It is frivolous to engage in browbeating, it doesn't work, and honestly, when people are forced into any behavior, the result are the illusion of change, a mirage. Attempting to project your will onto another is selfish, arrogant, and narcissistic behavior.

Accountability is simply put, owning your shit. While we have been sold the concept of "free speech," every word we speak costs us something. In our "microwave society," where everyone is quick to judge and offer their two cents in any matter, very few choose to take responsibility for the things they utter. In a world where attention is a new drug, often, many are craving their next fix. Despite the clear knowledge that the Internet is ever present, so many opt to share their opinion, using their words, to get across a point that may not necessarily need to be proven or otherwise.

While we may all be looking for someone to blame, very often, the culprit is in our own home, and we look at them every morning when we look in the mirror. Despite how easy it may be to blame society for our collective shortcomings, we do not give it credit when we go viral for uttering what is often nonsense. I know it's your opinion, and of course, it is of insurmountable value to you. There are instances where what comes up does not have to come out. One can be perceived as a fool, but the mystery is revealed with a simple conversation.

I am a firm believer that when it comes to making statements, whether they are written on social media or said during a conversation, they are placed in an email for all to see. My process has always been to run it through upstairs before I bring it downstairs for presentation. The trouble with saying "whatever we want" is that just because we have an intention, perception is always in the room. When it comes to expressing our thoughts or feelings, little to no adherence is given to the masses. Although we have the liberty of saying whatever we want to say, we are unable to shout fire in a public place due to the possibility of inciting a stampede. Often, when we are expressing ourselves, as defined within our inalienable rights, tact is lost.

Ownership is an amazing thing that should not be limited to material things. We are entitled to own our thoughts as they are in our heads. We are held accountable for our actions, which, more times than not, do not involve others, yet we are slow to hold each other accountable for the things that are said. Why do we have such a problem with holding ourselves accountable for the things that we say? Why is it that we are all so eager to drop our self-proclaimed jewels and gems, yet we are oblivious to owning the nuggets? Part of the reason that we refuse to own the things that we say, in my opinion, is due to restrictions imposed upon us at a very early age. In an attempt to correct a parental "wrong," the flood gates are open for everyone to share what grinds their gears, no matter who it offends.

I am the last person to impose upon anyone's right to disclose their opinion on any topic on which they are knowledgeable. However, I am the first one to reach out to those in my circle to correct or confirm. I believe that there is a fear that is running rampant in society. The notion that everyone can say whatever they want to say without consequence yet hides themselves behind the notion of free speech. My take is if you say it, and you mean it, and it is not mirroring verbal emotion, then stand on business.

Wisdom is more than a tooth. Wisdom should be the "guest" in every conversation where there is a free exchange of thoughts and opinions. It should be the scale that provides balance to any debate or disagreement. Although wisdom is not something that can be purchased, it is, in fact, the quality of having knowledge, experience, and good judgment.

Those who are wise are more likely to hold themselves accountable for the things that come out of their mouths. Since wisdom is accrued through knowledge, experience, and good judgment, it is safe to assume that these individuals have been around long enough to have learned through experiences that have shaped their moral fiber. Although there are some who would like to partner wisdom with maturity, I would strongly disagree.

When discussing wisdom, I would be remiss if I did not bring to light the proverbial "old fool" and "young dummy." The differences between the two are stupidity and ignorance. Regarding the "old fool," those individuals likely know better yet have chosen to not do better, possibly to dispel the possibility of anyone's expectations. On the other hand, a "young dummy" is very likely to have no good sense to make better decisions or exercise good judgment.

I make no attempt to be forgiving towards either party because we are bombarded with varying knowledge during this Information Age. Thanks to the Internet, which, in my opinion, is both a gift and a curse, we have access to things that we have never known and may never have known prior to the creation of the super information highway. When it comes to the smorgasbord or buffet of information that is readily available to us, we must determine what is good for us and what is bad. In reviewing all the information, both good and bad, it is no wonder "Alice" is in "Wonderland."

Naivety is what is displayed by many when the choice is made to use the tongue as a sword and a weapon. We are responsible for what we take in with our eyes and ears and what we put out with our mouths. No one wants the "credit" for making outlandish allegations or statements unless the results go viral, hence feeding the need for attention. The issue with going viral for making costly free speech is one very few are able to handle. If you do not have a team of people to assist in such situations, the results can vary between being canceled or physically harmed, depending on the severity.

Being naïve does not exclude any individual who decides they want their 15 minutes from public recourse or private consequence. Many have made public apologies or private acknowledgments of wrongdoing, yet that does little to restore their integrity or character. Since most people do not have a PR team to shape their public statements or a team of writers to compose their day-to-day conversations, we oversee what comes out of their mouths. It is the burden of parents to establish the societal norms upon their children that render them productive members of society. If this stone is left unturned, parents are certain to turn out individuals with little to no couth or tact.

Yearning for confirmation and validation are the people who lack accountability. Choosing that someone else's opinion of you trumps your own opinion. You are giving away something that you have worked for possibly years to accrue: your energy, your power. When giving away your power, your self-image, self-esteem, self-confidence, and self-worth become compromised.

When your view of yourself becomes distorted and watered down because you prioritized someone else's opinion, you relinquish your power and right to own your own opinion. You have chosen to abandon yourself for someone's reality and sacrifice the ability to hold yourself accountable. The adoption of someone else's thoughts paves the way for the mirroring of their words and actions, like a dummy.

When any individual yearns for the approval of others, they put themselves in a position where they are yielding their self-actualization. When you decide that the perception of your appearance decides how you feel on the inside, you become a puppet. Despite it being easier for some to follow than lead, the obligation of accountability is still applicable. While not everyone is born to lead, it is imperative that one never loses grasp of their self-concept.

Originals are more times than not of a greater value than duplicates when it comes to material things. The original is the first, the groundbreaker. Maybe it's me, but I don't remember the second person or persons to fly a plane. While I make no attempt to discourage modeling your life after that of another, it is my personal preference to make a footprint as opposed to following one. Despite the fact the road less traveled is daunting and inconvenient, the opportunity to carve a road that someone else may travel is fulfilling.

Accountability is the cornerstone of success and integrity. The absence of accountability is a breeding ground for chaos, confusion, and a lack of trust. To shy away from taking responsibility for your actions is hindering your own growth and undermining your progress. The adoption of accountability allows you to hold yourself to the highest standards, admit mistakes openly regardless of judgment, and actively seek solutions rather than placing blame. It takes courage and boldness to take ownership when things go wrong. You earn respect and build credibility when you embrace accountability with zeal; it is the foundation upon which true leadership is built.

Take Back Your Power

Learning, acknowledging, and remedying your flaws or shortcomings puts you at an advantage. By accepting that you are imperfectly perfect, no flaw you possess can be used against you. Words can, and do, hurt people to the extent that they leave emotional scars. When deciding to do shadow work to find out what makes you tick, you take away the advantage of the deceitful.

When you allow the words of others to dictate your reality, you are relinquishing your power. By giving away your power, you become a spectator in your own life. You have moved from the driver's seat to the passenger's seat without direction and destination. You are lost in all sense of the word. To allow an individual to shape your reality with their thoughts, words, and actions, in short, you have given them the right to alter your life. Once a person finds out how to "get your goat," they're always going to come for it. You have given them the rights to your life story, and you go from being the writer and creator to a role player.

People will project their insecurities and shortcomings onto you to have someone to look down on. What's weird is that due to their ego, often, people are operating from a place of some area of self-consciousness due to possible childhood trauma or just constant consumption of social media, and measure their success within the margins of others. In my experience, wounded people either take on the role of people pleasers or verbal aggressors with derogatory feedback for any conversation. What's unfortunate is that hurt people hurt people, and even when presented with an opportunity to heal, the addiction to attention supersedes the desire to be better. More times than not, a person will willfully disclose their intentions in any aspect of engagement, but if their actions do not align with the intentions presented, they likely have an underlying agenda; the energy they operate in will reveal their true intentions or their agenda. Sometimes, people will listen to your dreams, ambitions, and aspirations and talk them right out of fruition.

When a negative thought arises, immediately think about something positive, which changes your mood, subsequently giving you a "fresh set of eyes" or mindset to look at what got you upset. By looking at the situation with a new mind or positive mind, you are increasing the possibility of walking away with the new knowledge or lesson the situation introduced for that growing moment.

Teaching moments stem from growing moments, but you must choose growth and dismiss the negative train of thought. A negative train of thought can take one simple negative thought, the lead car of a train, infecting all the other cars and subsequently sending your thoughts, the proverbial train, off track. Off-track thoughts are a breeding ground for a negative attitude, deflecting your own misguided thoughts and feelings, with the end result being one person infecting others around them and only finding solace and comfort after releasing negativity into the air.

To walk away with the lesson in any given situation of engagement with others, you must assert the desire and claim the opportunity for growth. Despite the inconvenience of the occurrence presented, we must normalize the opportunity that stems from painful or hurtful interactions. Even when growth is forced upon us, we must seize the circumstances that can lead to success. Life creates challenges that are stepping stones for elevation, and only through focus and faith do they become recognizable. There are many instances where we get so consumed by what happened that we do not see what is happening. Life is full of distractions, which come in many forms.

Distractions are sometimes the people in our lives, circumstances we encounter when we map out plans and get busy making them happen, or we can be the distraction by getting in our own way, allowing fear to dictate our next step or lack thereof; imagine experiencing them all at once. Just as exercising at the gym strengthens our physical muscles, self-awareness strengthens our spirit, mind, and body. Because mental health is health, we must buy into the concept that all illness starts with our thoughts, which spill over into our words, subsequently poisoning our actions.

In casual conversations, we often hear the terms "accountability" and "power" thrown around without much thought. By delving deeper, we get an understanding that these concepts are critical in shaping our engagement and relationships with others. Accountability means taking responsibility for our thoughts, actions, and words and acknowledging our role in both success and failure. It requires honesty, integrity, and a willingness to learn from mistakes.

The power we have refers to the ability to influence others' behaviors or decisions. It can be used responsibly to empower those around us or misused to manipulate and control. Understanding how accountability and power intersect is key to equitable relationships. When holding ourselves accountable and being mindful of how we use our power, we wield positive changes and foster trust among individuals and our community.

Bridge or Ramp

During your engagement with others, their actions will let you know if they will serve as a bridge or a ramp in your life. To put it plainly, some people are the allies that will serve as the connections that lead us to new opportunities and new circumstances or earn their place in our cheering section. The opposite are those who will play the part of adversaries. These people will likely enter your life as the disruptors who will teach you lessons, forging those experiences that are likely painful but necessary for growth. The ramp people introduce deceit and deceptions that are intricate parts of our growth that foster lifelong lessons that we will share with others with the hopes of preventing them from learning the hard way. While we are not all teachers or leaders, the inconvenience of the offence we experience makes way for the opportunity to be of service, perhaps, to someone in our cheering section or on our respective journeys.

By opting for kindness, no matter the intention of others, we ignite a flow of positive energy that vibrates from the inside out. When projecting what you're expecting to receive in return, you get an opportunity to see whether a person is a bridge or a ramp; actions are always telling. While I would never advise walking into any situation with expectations because that is the fast track to disappointment, it is okay to desire to receive what you give in any given situation. The priority is to not put yourself in a situation where your desires are unrealistic when a person has already shown you who they are. Because people are creatures of habit and old habits die hard, change, though necessary, is a pain that many people avoid. Some resist change, viewing it as an unwelcome burden, perhaps due to past failures and negative reactions. People choose comfort to avoid someone's hypercritical judgement. We must get busy prioritizing what we want, how we feel, and what we expect from ourselves. You only live once, so why not be the star of your own show. Choose change, move in silence, and celebrate yourself when no one else restores your faith, self-love, and peace of mind.

The key to finding inner peace and connecting deeply within is to find and recognize your ego and then reject it. Acceptance plays an important part in your spiritual growth. When you really care about your progression, it will happen. Your inner peace will be realized once the change occurs from deep within. Cease your investment in those who are negative, discourage change, or make attempts to dismantle you; the investment of time and energy in these people must cease. Collectively, we must stop the behavior of investing time in people and circumstances where we are not getting a positive return. This is the equivalent of depositing money in a bank where there are always insufficient funds; close out the engagement just as you would close out that account.

Life's A Stage, Cast With Caution

Life is indeed a stage. In any play I have seen, live or televised, I innately pay attention to the cast and their roles. Often, in my head, I recast for my own satisfaction, but that's the director in me. Throughout our lives, we cast people for the various roles that are within our control. Family, for example, is what we are born into and not able to choose. I do not believe this to be true because there are countless instances where friends can become family and family can become estranged. No matter the case, friends can be more supportive, loving, and consistent than family; the objective is to surround yourself with people who will propel the locomotive that is you. With the same token, some family members choose to disown or disavow for their own reasons, negative or positive, that vary from justified to nonsensical but may be logical overall to the disowner.

Life is like a never-ending Broadway show, full of unexpected plot twists and rotating cast members. Just when you think you've got the script memorized, in comes a curveball and suddenly you're scrambling to improvise. Change is the backstage crew sneaking in during intermission and switching up the set design without warning. It keeps us on our toes and forces us to adapt, to grow, and to evolve. Embracing chaos is a part of what makes a good show a great show. Since every action does not warrant a reaction, when we slow down to get the necessary guidance and intuition, we are able to see the wrong thing from a mile away. Intuition is us throwing caution to the wind, following divine signs, ensuring that at any given time, we are exactly where we are supposed to be, no matter where we THINK we should be. Life may be a stage, but that doesn't mean you can't steal the show every now and then and be led before leading.

Change and accountability go hand in hand. As we navigate through the twists and turns of our existence, we are constantly faced with choices that shape our path and impact those around us. Without accountability, it's easy to slip into an indifferent mindset, blaming others for our failures or avoiding responsibility altogether. When we hold ourselves accountable for our actions, we take ownership of our lives and empower ourselves to make positive changes. It's all about being honest, acknowledging mistakes, and striving to do better in the future. Once the change occurs, remember that accountability is not about self-blame but rather a tool for growth and self-improvement. Embrace it, learn from it, and watch how your perspective on life shifts for the better.

While engaging with others, accountability and change are two essential components for fostering personal growth. The former ensures that we take ownership of our actions, decisions, and outcomes. By holding ourselves accountable, we demonstrate our commitment to values, resulting in a more cohesive and proactive society.

Embracing change is crucial for adapting to evolving ways of thinking, advancements in successful communication, and acknowledgment of individual needs. By being open to change and willing to learn new skills and strategies, we can position ourselves as adaptable and forward-thinking leaders. Ultimately, by combining accountability with a willingness to adapt and grow, we can drive positive change within ourselves to foster our long-term success.

Chapter Four

NAVIGATION

Navigating change can be a tricky thing, like trying to find your way through a maze without a map. It's normal to feel overwhelmed or uncertain when faced with new situations or unexpected shifts in life. However, embracing change leads to growth and opportunities for personal development. The key is to approach it with an open mind and a willingness to adapt. Take things one step at a time, focusing on what you can control and letting go of what you can't. Remember that it's okay to ask for help or seek guidance from others who have been through similar experiences. Change may not always be easy, but it can ultimately lead you down a path toward something better and brighter. Just keep moving forward, stay positive, and trust in your ability to handle whatever comes your way.

Emotions can be messy and overwhelming to navigate, but it's an essential part of life. It's important to remember that all emotions are valid, even the negative ones. The key is to acknowledge what you're feeling, without judgment, and then figure out why you're feeling that way. Is it because of something external or internal? Once you pinpoint the source of your emotions, you can start to work through them in a healthy way. This might involve talking to someone you trust, practicing self-care activities like exercise or meditation, or simply giving yourself time to process and reflect. It's okay to own your feelings and seek help if you need it. Emotions are complicated, but navigating them with grace and self-compassion can lead to growth and resilience in the long run.

It's amazing how the things we see as inconveniences in our lives are divine detours. They are God-created opportunities for growth and prosperity that, more times than not, involve being of service to others. When we veer off "our plans," we tend to get distracted by the inconvenience of not being able to carry out something that may not have been a part of our destiny. The objective is to set our plans and allow God to order our steps. For instance, we put directions in a GPS and trust an electronic device to guide us to where we're going; that's a lot of trust in technology. Technology has failed me on uncountable times, but God hasn't failed me once.

As a big-picture person, it humbles me how every time I experience what many view as an inconvenience and converts it into an opportunity to be of service to someone who needs help. In the past, I would be so busy bitching and complaining about the inconvenience, the time lost, and having to plan a different route that I would never see the opportunity; a change in my way of thinking revealed a whole new path for me. By prioritizing what I thought should be happening and how I felt like things would unfold, I forced God and faith to the bleachers while I was the superstar, getting everything and nothing done. The results of my works, without my faith, are the equivalent of running on a hamster wheel. I was tired since things were getting done, but no progress was being made. It was at that point that many things came to my realization that I needed to slow down and take stock of my life.

With the knowledge that time is borrowed and not promised, and it's the one thing that we haven't figured out how to get more of, I decided a change needed to happen in my life. I consider myself to be in possession of above-average intelligence but the way I was choosing to live my life was quite the contrary. I was making moves, but I wasn't getting anywhere. Being set in your ways is an ugly thing when you see that the reality you saw was not the one that existed. I was navigating like a person with all the intention and no "proper guidance," but it looked good from the outside. I began to see that most of the moves I was making were to please people. I was walking country miles for people who wouldn't jump off their front porch for me. While this was disheartening, I allowed myself enough time to reflect on how I was feeling and move on to repair my relationship with myself and rebuild the one with my God. In choosing to change, I reaffirmed something I had always said to others: people are creatures of habit, and old habits die hard.

In deciding to move differently, I expected to lose some people in my life; it was par for the course. When you decide to change, your circle of friends, family, and associates becomes very telling. How you navigate after the loss of people is paramount to how consistent you are with your decision. It's easy to fall back into old habits and behaviors because of the comfort. Comfort has killed more dreams than procrastination; let that sink in. The literal sentiment of that statement is basically that being content with something is the fastest way to miss out on something better. To deprive yourself of growth, elevation, and ascension should be criminal. Still, many choose comfort because of fear.

Fear breeds anxiety, which propels a reality that does not exist, but what we feed is what grows. Hence, fear sprouting legs, walking down, and dousing everything that could have been; that's murder. In most instances, despite being the co-creators of our realities with God, many will point the finger at others for their lack of success or the obliteration of their dreams and endeavors, that is the farthest thing from the truth. We choose to be victims by blaming someone else for our decisions not to proceed in any endeavor that we planned in our minds that does not come to fruition. Being a victim is a choice because it is our train of thought that is derailed by the expectations of others.

We have become so jaded collectively when it comes to the victim mentality that we don't want to admit to being victimized but we'll take empathy, sympathy, or attention from others that tends to accompany a misfortune. It is easy to focus on the mishap because it is happening at that opportune moment, and of course, since the objective is to "be present" at the moment, it never crosses one's mind how long to marinate on the malfeasance possibly caused by another. We want immediate support for our desired revenge or retribution. We exclaim, "we have been wronged," and only vengeance will make it right. By accepting "unacceptable" behavior as a character trait, we deprive ourselves of an opportunity for self-evaluation or growth, dwindling the possibility that these issues will be addressed. There is a root cause to every character flaw, and we must choose to take the opportunity to do the bit of work and digging if we want to change, grow, elevate, and evolve. The opportunity for growth is either chosen or chucked, there's no in between.

Inconveniences Are Opportunities in Work Clothes

When we spend time alone, that is when we get to know ourselves best. We take the opportunity to pull out the mirror and take a long, hard look at our shortcomings, our flaws, our insecurities, our finer points, those things that flatter, and our confidence. It is only through knowledge of ourselves that we can notice opportunities amid inconvenience. The steps must be taken to get to know ourselves to be certain that the opinions we speak are ours, founded by our facts and research, not a regurgitation of someone else's synopsis. One of the easiest things in the world is to be fed. You don't have to worry about using your hands to touch and eyes to read, you just need ears to hear; you don't even have to understand it. To so many people, repeating the thoughts of someone else, verbatim, is a lesson that they have studied well. This could not be further from the truth.

When choosing the role of an understudy, you have decided that living in the shadows of someone else is your lot in life; that is a very peculiar choice. As an understudy, you may never get a chance to see the stage, but you will have years and years to study under the star. You may not even be the only understudy. The question is, how will you ever get what is for you when you are standing in the shadows of someone else's shine? If you choose to be ordinary, no rippling of the water, going along to get along, and choosing silence in pivotal moments of your life, you will never know how extraordinary you could be. If this is a role you have decided to take, regret at the end of the day is almost a certainty. Voluntarily getting into a car with someone you know, not asking about the destination, not asking questions during unplanned detours, and allowing yourself to be led is people-pleasing. Your higher power should be the only source with access and authority to your morale and character. People are corrupted by power; the more you give them, the more they want. Despite opportunities to build character, some people choose manipulation. While this is a poor reflection on their character, it's unfortunate that if character were currency, the majority would be bankrupt.

Life is full of inconveniences and opportunities. If we allow ourselves to lose sight of the totality of any given situation, out the door goes reason and rational. When inconveniences rear their ugly heads, because we are so focused on our plan, our agenda, and what we want to transpire, we do not see that something better and more beneficial has arisen. The first step is acknowledging that what has happened is not the end all be all but a minor distraction. Inconveniences can be viewed as a distraction. Their sole purpose is to distract to draw your attention to something better, not anger or wrong emotion. It is divine because it is redirecting you to the purposeful path that has been previously ordained for you. Just as you are running late, and you never run late, the minor inconvenience gives you the grand opportunity to miss a 4-car pile-up with fatalities in the rain. We have become so committed to the hustle and bustle that the notion of slow and steady is a thing of the past.

It is our intention, in any given circumstance, that, when coupled with the expectations we impose upon ourselves, contributes to the layout of our reality. In shaping our reality, we must be willing to be ever-changing and welcome growth. Growth is intricate when thinking about change and opportunities because being complacent is stifling. Choosing to remain stagnant is the equivalent of chaining yourself to a boulder and walking in place for the rest of your life. We have been growing since we were babies. From the voluntary decision to walk and run, no one chose the pain of teeth violently ripping through our gums, but are we not grateful for the growing pains and suffering, all in the name of change and growth? We are responsible for creating our own reality. You can choose to live in your head, where it's comfortable, but regret is a big price to pay for a living as an understudy.

Life Experiences

Our intentions mark our life experiences. The instances when we have good intentions that craft how we experience our day-to-day lives. Life, like an onion, stinks to some but is interesting to some degree to all. Our intention, our reasoning behind our thoughts, actions, and words, weave a sophisticated tapestry. Depending on our history with some and our experiences with others, our intentions are either seeded or rooted. If seeded, our intentions mirror our agenda and are innocent, honest, pure, and natural. Seeded intentions are those that are bred from what most people consider to be "our first mind," the voice in our head, or the voice of God. It is believed to be our true response, without emotions.

Rooted intentions are a bit more mature. They have been shaped by experience that changed the foundation by shifting it and causing disruption. They are poisoned by our emotions that were allowed to fester because they were never dispelled. While each emotion does not have to be felt in the moment, we should allow ourselves the opportunity to grieve the moment that we felt offended, give ourselves grace, extend grace to the offender, release the offense, and decide our relationship with that individual moving forward. It may not sound that simple to apply in the moment but when we decided to walk, we didn't give up after the first day or the first fall.

We own the rights to our expectations. We are responsible for our expectations. We should collectively refrain from showing up with our expectations, laying them at the mercy of another person whom we cannot control, and choosing to be disappointed because OUR expectations were not met. Expectations are basically the results we desire in any given situation, engagement, circumstance, or matter. Unless you are the only person involved, each situation would have the opportunity to write its own history. Walking into a situation where there is another individual with feelings, thoughts, and emotions, presenting your expectations is a bit selfish and arrogant. Expectations have caused plenty of arguments and have lost plenty of fights. Many would argue that you are entitled to your expectations. Yes, but you are also responsible for them. Everyone wants to bring them, but no one wants to be responsible for them. It's like bringing kids to a party for adults. You decide to bring them but don't want to be responsible for them; you'll end up disappointed if there isn't a place for them.

Reality is our life experiences, the various levels we embark upon as we proceed on our journey. During our lives, we fortify ourselves for various outcomes, instances, and possibilities that may never come. We wander so far down the road of what-ifs that we miss the shortcuts to opportunities. We've devised a plan where giving up is okay as long as you thought it out as far as you could have. It is irrational to allow a dream to die at its onset because of imaginable, created obstacles that may never see the light of day and, quite frankly, may never materialize. The reality of self-defeat and self-sabotage is a bewildering existence. It is bewildering in the sense that a person would choose to be so cavalier about their life and reality and take such an elementary route towards growth and progress. It is in these instances when a person awakens to the idea of having abandoned the ship and allowing pirates to take over that the line between the agenda and the intention becomes blurred.

The agenda is the reasoning for a person's words or actions. Whether that agenda be to aid, to learn, to deceive, or to take, it traditionally mirrors the intention, unless rooted and drenched in past life—basically negative. When it comes to reality, agendas emerge as close relative to intentions. In most circumstances, the agenda and intention are one and the same. I will admit that after living a bit of life, the preceding statement does not always ring true. During my engagements and interactions with people, there have been occurrences when the agenda was akin to the intention or far removed from it. It is the instances where I was on the receiving end of a situation, the agenda was presented, but the intentions, not in alignment with the agenda, were revealed by God, yep, good old-fashioned deception.

While I haven't been deceived much or often, everyone has their opportunity to prove themselves prudent and trustworthy; I'm a fast learner or a quick read. I allow the energy of a person to let me know their intentions. Before a word is uttered, I remain quiet to sense the deception or lack thereof. We all consist of energy; this is a difficult concept for most people to wrap their heads around. If a person enters a room and can change the vibe in the room, that's some powerful energy. Just as a person sucks the fun out of the room with their presence or energy alone, equally powerful but in a different way. Over years of building bridges, relationships, or grudges for some people, through discernment and intuition, you can sense the energy of an individual and proceed with caution. Men lie, women lie, energy doesn't.

Life experiences and change go hand in hand, like peanut butter and jelly, except no one really knows which one is which. Change is inevitable like that awkward phase in middle school where you were convinced neon braces were cool. It's the life experiences that shape us into the fabulous messes we are today. Whether falling headfirst into a relationship or face-planting into a new job, every stumble and triumph carve out our story. Embrace chaos because, without it, we would all be as bland as unsalted crackers. As a rule of thumb, when life throws you a curveball, and it will, just remember to swing for the fences with style and finesse because, at the end of the day, those are the moments that make us who we are.

Conscious Release

Every time we repeat a story that makes us feel bad or causes a negative response, we are mentally revisiting that situation and experience all the same feelings that were introduced in that moment. By constantly revisiting a negative event, we increase the possibility of negative situations with a jaded mindset. We must live in that moment, learn in that moment, and move from that moment. It is mentally unproductive and toxic to hold on to negativity, anger, frustration, or any emotional response that does not propel you towards growth or change positively. Just as we purge through our things when we move from one place to another, we must purge our thoughts, which cleanses our emotional palate and fosters the environment for positive actions.

Conscious release and change are elusive concepts akin to Batman and Robin; they are essential partners. The elusive concept is like trying to catch a unicorn in a field of rainbows—whimsical and mysterious, yet undeniably powerful. Picture this: you finally let go of all those negative thoughts swirling around your mind like a tornado, and suddenly, you feel as light as a feather drifting through the wind. That's the magic of conscious release. By acknowledging our emotions, facing our fears head-on, and choosing to let go of what no longer serves us, we open ourselves up to transformation and growth. It's like cleaning our soul—tossing out old beliefs and behaviors that weigh us down and making room for new beginnings. So next time you're feeling stuck in a rut, remember the power of conscious release and change; it might just be the key to unlocking your true potential.

Meditation

Meditation is something as simple as the prayer

that we say over our food before consumption. It is as simple as giving thanks as you awake in the morning for a day not promised using time that is borrowed. Meditation is merely taking time to reflect on the moment in the moment and acknowledging appreciation. One may choose to meditate in a manner that removes any negative energy that affects the whole day. During meditation, you must release the negative energy to allow positive energy to enter, which, if projected outward consistently, returns twofold, allowing the manifestation of positive thoughts, feelings, and actions.

Meditation is like hitting the refresh button on your brain, giving you the tools to navigate the tumultuous waters of change with grace and ease. By quieting the mind and tuning into our inner selves, we can unlock a sense of calm that allows us to approach life's inevitable changes with equanimity. Through meditation, we learn to let go of resistance and embrace opportunity, viewing change as an exciting adventure rather than a daunting challenge. By meditating regularly, we nurture a mindset that is flexible and resilient, able to adapt to whatever curveballs life throws our way with a wink and a smile. So next time you find yourself amid upheaval, grab your meditation cushion and remember change is just another chance to show off your Zen mastery.

Change is inevitable, like a bad haircut from the 90s that you just can't seem to forget. But it's all about how you approach it. You can either embrace it like a fearless warrior ready to conquer new challenges or resist it like a stubborn mule clinging to outdated ways of thinking. Trust me, nobody wants to be known as the person still using a flip phone in 2025. So, shake off that old mentality like last season's fashion trends and adopt a growth mindset. Embrace change with open arms and a witty sense of humor because, let's face it, life is too short to be stuck in the past. Plus, who knows what exciting opportunities could be lurking around the corner waiting for you to seize the day: carpe diem.

Chapter Five

GRACE

Being patient with myself and giving myself grace was the hardest part of changing for me. It was easier to forgive others of indiscretions and offenses upon me than to forgive myself. To say that out loud now sounds weird to me; the revelation of this behavior in myself was quite daunting. My rationale for the behavior boiled down to my unwillingness to set boundaries to avoid confrontation. I am not a confrontational person, nor am I meek; I just decided at some point that every action does not deserve a reaction. I figured out that there are tests that we encounter in life that lead us to certain character developmental stages and growth. I was so busy, in so many instances, falling on my sword to keep the peace, I was losing my peace. I was so focused on rushing to resolve matters to move forward that I realized I had chained a boulder to my ankle and was walking in circles.

I committed to a behavior that left me stagnant, reliving the same cycle over and over again. I was passive about many things and passionate about even fewer; I was running in place; I was a hamster. When I decided to change, I began to see all the things I had done in so many situations that exposed me on so many levels, and no one cared, not even me. I wasn't upset with the offenders; I was upset with myself because I felt like a people-pleasing pushover. I had become so inactive in the present moment that I likely just checked out because I was bored; finding my passion became my mission. With prayer, persistence, and patience, I got better and better at giving myself grace for what happened and what was happening. I decided to control what I could and release the rest; it was liberating.

Removing your expectations from situations is key to releasing and letting go. While there are some situations where life-changing decisions are at play, of course, we are very invested in those conversations collectively; however, that's not the case in most conversations. I was guilty of over-investing in situations, people, circumstances, and places. Expectations arise when we invest in situations, people, or results we are unable to control fully or consistently, unknown variable. Like the lottery, you can't control the draw, so you don't play, hence, no disappointment because there was no investment. We must give people the room to be who they have shown themselves to be and not impose OUR expectations upon them, injecting the possibility of disappointment. Accountability in any disagreement warrants grace to all parties involved, but you must plant the seed and foster its growth to ensure consistency and graduation into a habit.

Grace is an important part of change. It is important in the sense that, theoretically, by forgiving yourself, it becomes easier to forgive others. To move forward, you must allow the wound or affliction to heal. If the wound does not heal, it becomes infected and spreads. Similarly, emotions need to be expressed. When we hold things in and choose not to feel or voice the emotions in the moment, we create a circumstance where they snowball. If we do not release our emotions and feelings, we run the risk of emotions compounding and pressure building and we unload or explode over something small. You now have to be accountable or accusatory because you chose not to feel and move forward. Are you going to take the blame or place the blame?

Moments like these build character where apologizing is the best thing to do, and you sort it out with yourself immediately afterward. Holding yourself accountable in that moment, you choose to initiate the change you want to see. You are negating the offense that has occurred by transforming that inconvenience into an opportunity for growth. By consciously deciding to transmute the negative circumstances, energy, thoughts, and actions, we assert that we possess the emotional intelligence to change the dynamic of any situation that drains our positivity. The act of asserting our power to regain or maintain control of ourselves in any situation is a step towards the change that we should all want to see.

Access Your Power to Propel Change

I am a firm believer that with the 3 P's anything is possible. Applying prayer, persistence, and patience will make anything possible and attainable. I am proof that when we abandon caution for risk, fear takes a back seat to the pursuit of our passions. Accepting that failure can happen should not serve as a deterrent but as motivation to invoke the trial-and-error method in any situation. Failure shows us what didn't or won't work, propelling the desire to keep going and figure out the proper path to our pursuits. Failure can be a blessing in disguise; any rejection is divine protection.

Prayer Leads the Train to Change

Acknowledging a being, spirit, or entity exists provides a path to seek guidance, comfort, and strength in times of need. Many believe that positive change can be brought about in their lives and the world around them through prayer. In the pursuit of the road to forgiveness, healing, or clarity on a decision, prayer can provide a sense of peace and hope. Collectively, people view prayer as a way to connect with a higher power or a form of meditation or reflection. Regardless of the circumstance, the act of prayer has been shown to have powerful effects on individuals' mental and emotional well-being. When using prayer to set intentions and focus on positive outcomes, we can experience shifts in attitudes and actions that result in meaningful change in our lives.

Prayer is the guardrail that keeps persistence and patience on track. When we choose to pray, theoretically, our loads should get lighter, we should gain clarity, and we should be able to maintain or gather focus; I repeat theoretically. People will pray and still choose to worry about the outcome of a situation, the person who has committed the offense, or just general concern for the matter at hand. Since we are creatures of habit and do not see the entity we are praying to, we tend to give away the problem and hold fast to the worry. No matter how often we hear, "you can't have faith and worry," the behavior remains unchanged. How can we see the change when we have decided to stand in its way?

Very few things materialize in the form we expect, which means we often miss the answered prayer. Faith does not permit the hands-on creation of our desired response; faith ensures that our prayers are answered in a way conducive to our destiny. The response is tailored in a manner that sometimes there are things that we must do to unveil, reveal, or expose the path set forth before us. If we pray for a car and are presented with a person who sells discounted cars, or we are gifted a car with a balance that we must pay off and given a better-paying job, is that not the answer to your prayers? Some would say no because, despite the general nature of their request, the desire was not satisfied. We often end up disappointed because we do not get what we asked for, but we are supplied with what we need. Miracles happen every day, but sometimes, we are so hinged on the tailoring of the answered prayer with the wires of our expectations that we lose sight of victory because of our mindset. Change starts with our minds.

Prayer takes our trust out of the hands of people and places it on the shoulders of faith. Faith is essentially forgetting about it to heal. When we invite faith into any circumstance where we have exhausted our natural responses, the supernatural will always prevail. We must release our control and let go of our expectations because when we do not get what is expected, faith is weakened and our train of thought could derail or, worse, expedited to a negative track.

By adopting the attitude that if something does not work out in our favor, there must be something bigger and better coming, we establish the positivity needed to propel our mental state. Taking on the attitude that "if at first we don't succeed, try, try, again" provides the soil that will allow the planting of our deepest desires and goals that are to be cultivated, fostered, and sprout into fruition. We determine how much we fail by how hard and how often we try. By getting knocked down nine times and getting up ten, we build the parachute that will carry us to our desired goals with a bit of turbulence and strong winds but resting safely at the destination.

Persistence Keeps the Choo-Choo, Choo-Chooing

Persistence and change are kindred spirits; one propels the other on the same course. Persistence is the key to achieving goals and overcoming challenges. It is par for the course when it comes to the effective cultivation of change. By sticking to our guns, staying determined, and not giving up when things get tough, we are certain to obtain any and every goal we pursue.

Change is an inevitability when it comes to calculating the formula for growth. Adapting to new circumstances is essentially learning from our mistakes and being open to considering and enacting new approaches. Creating a balance between persistence and change is necessary for our pursuits for success; trust the process. The balance between persistence and change looks like pushing forward with determination and pivoting in a different direction, if necessary; it's a divine detour. In this way, we can actively navigate through the twists and turns of life, progressing toward our dreams and aspirations.

Persistence is a key to introducing change and chartering the course. Setbacks and obstacles are natural occurrences along the way, however, staying committed and persevering will ultimately lead to success. Determination and perseverance are crucial to breaking a bad habit, learning a new skill, or making a major life change. Change takes time, effort, and dedication; it won't happen overnight. You must be prepared for a journey you planned but must maintain persistence to complete it despite the obstacles; faith comes in handy at this time. Bumps in the road occur to determine if you are serious about the change; don't let them discourage you from continuing your path. Adjustments will be needed, but we must stay focused on the end goal; it helps when you can see what you're working for. Persistence and resilience are intricate players when overcoming any challenges that come your way.

Persistence and patience go together like cheese and crackers, like Scooby-Doo and Shaggy, like ketchup and mustard. Persistence is getting knocked down seven times and getting up eight. It is your commitment to something that will better you in the long run, so you must reap it so you can sow. Patience is not the easiest, especially when you have been overcome by adversity and obstacles; it is necessary to persevere and not give up. When we are busy focusing on what happened in any situation and lose sight of the shore, we are easily deterred and prone to give in because we have given out. The test is not giving up on the destination but revising the journey. Persistence greases the wheels on the journey towards change.

Essential components for personal growth and development are patience, persistence, and change.

It is the virtuous nature of patience that allows us to endure difficulties with grace and composure while understanding that progress takes time. Change doesn't happen overnight, so it's important to remember that patience with yourself is key. The driving force behind making positive changes in our lives is persistence. Persistence requires dedication and determination to keep pushing forward even when faced with obstacles. Embracing the challenge of change is necessary for growth and self-improvement. By combining patience, persistence, and change, we can navigate life's ups and downs with resilience, adaptability, and a positive attitude. Practicing patience, persistence, and openness to change will lead us toward a happier, more fulfilling life.

Patience Greases the Wheels of Change

Change is a process that paves the way for challenges, healing, accountability, and grace. The challenge is to let go of old pains, heal from the hurts, accept what you could have done differently, and forgive yourself to move forward and grow. Emotional wounds linger, get infected, infect others, and spread if we don't allow ourselves to heal. Learning to release the pain and forgiving the offense can be difficult. However, it will always be worth it. Healing isn't selfish, but you must prioritize your journey to succeed. You must trust the process to be tailored to your needs, desires, strengths, and emotions. There is no comparison to someone else because of different destinations.

During the healing process, we forgive others and release negative energy, avoiding negative emotions. Negative emotions lay the foundation for negative thoughts, fostering the growth of negative actions. When we decide to concede, we regain the focus on our present by laying the past to rest and making way for the future. The times we dwell on what was, we open the door to depression, however, too much focus on the future breeds anxiety. Today is all we have because time is borrowed, not promised; we have an opportunity to change every day; it's a choice. Healing is what we owe ourselves, and it's a win-win situation.

The road to redemption and resolve is smoother when we are willing to admit our fault in situations with less-than-desirable results. The hardest thing for many people to do is to hold themselves accountable for any behavior or reaction that ran the train from the tracks. By conducting our train of thought, we may have periods of wavering, but things are always steady. When we become slow to anger and realize that, more times than not, nothing is the best thing to say and the best thing to do, the seed of peace is planted. Asserting our boundaries consistently shows others how we will be treated, and our peace is paramount, not to be taken lightly by anyone; teach people how to treat you.

Some people will reject the changes you make, the boundaries you impose, and the asserting of your power; their intentions are revealed because they differed from their agenda. Accountability starts at home and travels well when we extend grace. Because we are all in different phases of change and growth, if the engagement becomes a weight and not wealth, you are possibly dealing with a taker, not a giver. When we come to certain realities, no matter how long the relationship has existed, we must decide whether to release the person, place, or circumstance or suffer in silence, stimulating the growth of resentment and regret. While it is comfortable to expect someone to change or expect them to treat you differently without asserting your boundaries, you can expect disappointment to show up like clockwork. They are your expectations, and no one is obligated to fulfill them, and it will be your disappointment that you end up with. Accountability is an act of grace that navigates the positive energy generated by the clarity brought forth by honesty, forgiveness, and release.

Patience and change go hand in hand, like peas in a pod, overwhelming at times, causing anxiety and uncertainty. It is the strength our faith needs during periods of change that can make all the difference. Allowing things to unfold at their own pace allows us to adapt, grow, and embrace new possibilities. Patience is the calm anchor amidst the turbulence of change that aids navigation through challenges with grace and resilience. Patience gives us the freedom to approach transitions with an open mind and a positive attitude, trusting that good things take time to manifest. Consider if we never were tolerant enough as infants to sustain the push-through of teeth through our gums; painful but necessary. The next time you are amid change, take a deep breath, practice patience, and trust the process.

Patience is an important partner to change. Rarely does impatience lead to the desired outcome of success or change. Whether trying to develop a new habit, going through a career change, or navigating a challenging situation, rushing the process is a surefire way to end up at the corner of dissatisfaction and disappointment. Time and effort are required when on the road to change, so give yourself some grace if you don't see immediate results. Avoid frustration or giving up easily, and make a concerted effort to approach change with a sense of curiosity and openness. Embracing the journey and trusting that with consistency and perseverance, you will eventually reach your goals which motivates you to keep going, no matter what. Setbacks are a normal part of the process. Be gentle with yourself and acknowledge your progress; no matter how small, progress is progress. Set yourself up for long-term success and growth by practicing patience when choosing change.

If we were to accept that this moment was all we had, what would we do differently? Would the idea of having just this moment breed anxiety or ambition? Will you take the opportunity to plan and allow your steps to be ordered, or will you continue letting life happen and wonder why you're not getting what you want out of it? It can seem a bit odd to expect to get something out of nothing; you must give God something to work with. He gave us the gift, the passion, and the purpose; the least we can do is sit down long enough to map out the journey. Faith confirms your success; belief doesn't cost anything, but not believing costs so much more.

Often, we give the perseverance and patience of our prayers to others, neglecting ourselves. The love, patience, and consideration must start with the seeds we plant and foster into mature trees. The trees we plant extend the branches that cover and protect those placed on our paths and throughout our journey. While it is easy to spew the negative and maintain a negative attitude, consider the seeds you are planting in yourself and the fruit being cultivated. Sustaining a positive outlook, while challenging, is not impossible. The expectation of a happy day when you constantly reflect on what didn't happen and when it didn't happen is insanity. The life you lead will be filled with regret, disdain, piss, and vinegar; that's a tall order. Our words truly do build the houses we live in.

Chapter Six

ENERGY

If life were a machine, what would power it? Just like a car that needs fuel or electricity to move, the life machine needs to be powered. I believe it would be our energy that powers it. Would that motivate people to live or lead more positive, happy lives? Would people be more honest, more trustworthy, more transparent? Would people show up as their authentic selves at every opportunity because they realize that someone else's opinion of them is not their business?

What if this is the game of life and your energy powers it? Are you going to create the player you wish you were, or will you play as your authentic self? Will you pretend life's a stage and wear the mask that gives those you encounter comfort, but it gives you anxiety? Do you plan to make as much money as possible playing the game so the game doesn't play with you? With the knowledge that you can't borrow time, and it's not promised, what energy would power the game of your life?

I asked myself these questions when I realized there was time for a change in my life. My energy was so diluted and convoluted due to my priorities being off. I was people-pleasing, unintentionally, due to my lack of boundaries, discontent with confrontation, and my inability to consistently manage my emotions. Honestly, looking at the outside, people were impressed, but inside I was stressed. I was failing to be there for me, the most important person in my life.

While I do want everyone to win, I was literally building the dreams of others while watching mine die or be stifled, at the least. I was neglecting myself and unleashing unresolved emotion and negative energy in situations where the actual issue did not originate; I likely came across as unbalanced or unstable. I was allowing issues to snowball, only to melt in random places, soaking random people. Change was the best thing to ever happen to me. Choosing change was challenging, and trusting the process has been even harder, but through faith, prayer, persistence, and patience, I am so far removed from who I used to be and doing what I used to do. That is both joyous and frightening at the same time because people are creatures of habit, and my old habits were untethered, forcing me to make concerted efforts to maintain my new way of thinking and being, which subsequently changes my actions and engagements with others.

Because we are all works in progress, change does not necessarily come naturally for us all because comfort is what is normally sought. Once attained, the drive and determination to be better or evolve is slowed if not ceased. The way the game of life works, our opportunities for growth, expansion, and new levels are accomplished through challenges. We must step outside our comfort zones to encounter the complex and unknown to excel. By setting goals, instilling aspirations, and trying new things, we put forth the drive and perseverance necessary to better ourselves. When we decide we want to be better, persistence fuels the process, and positive energy propels us; negative energy promotes spiraling and anxiety. Learning to manage our emotions is imperative to change, succeed, level up, and grow.

Snatching Up the Carpet

Our emotions are a part of our foundation. With each experience we encounter, we have an opportunity to react, respond, or not; no reaction is a reaction. In preserving our positive energy, we must accept that not every action deserves a reaction and that the agenda and the intentions are not always the same when we engage with others. Because it is our energy, we are responsible for its maintenance. Theoretically, following the end of any relationship, whether business or personal, we should snatch up the carpet.

Snatching up the carpet is an emotional reset. During an emotional reset, I take some time and step away from my engagements and communications with others to give myself the opportunity to purge any residual or unprocessed emotion. The purpose of the purge is to ensure that your old, negative, misplaced energy is not carried into the new level or new opportunity. We purge ourselves of things when we move from one place to another, so why wouldn't we take the same approach when it comes to our mental health and well-being? I have found that when I step away to take emotional inventory, I give myself an opportunity to take stock of things in my life and to see missed opportunities or obstacles that arose that could have been handled differently.

My main purpose for taking stock is to hold myself accountable for any situations derailed because I was too emotionally invested or not invested enough to gain any wisdom or knowledge necessary for myself or someone I encounter. I firmly believe that the hardest lessons we must learn have the most tests; I welcome the challenge of change because that is where my growth hides. While there are those instances that, at first glance, can blind our judgment by repetition or reappearance, we are presented with the opportunity to get to the root of our response and possibly navigate to the necessary path that will lead to resolution and a new lesson. Because there is a need to see the circumstance with a fresh set of eyes upon each occurrence, our journey is more enriched with each step we take, no matter what the basis, with a lesson that will serve as wisdom to provide clarity that lasts a lifetime.

Taking Stock of Things

After clearing our emotional palates, we should use this opportunity to take stock. When taking stock, I take the opportunity to review my energetic consumption and my energetic distribution. While it may be more worthwhile and fulfilling to live a life as a giver, which is admirable, it is emotionally taxing and damaging due to the existence of energy vampires. I find it emotionally and energetically rewarding to be a reliable, helpful, attentive person who is good to have around, but I had to learn the hard way that some people are more attuned to the comfort of receiving. More times than not it is the comfort allotted by the giver that eventually transforms that helping hand into someone's crutch.

The part of taking stock that relates to your energetic consumption requires surveying your screen time on your phone and television; the music you listen to also impacts your energetic consumption. The things we see on television contribute to shaping our reality by spilling into our subconscious, mixing with our emotional responses, and subsequently emerging as our thoughts, choices, and opinions. If a person chooses to spend their days watching varying news channels all day, they will be prone to anxiety, paranoia, or depression because of the possible adaptation of the negative energy into their system. Just as varying media outlets can influence our energy and emotions, constant engagement with a negative person can have the same effect on our lives. It's easy to become someone's confidante or a "shoulder to cry on," but we must make a concerted effort to help without harm to ourselves. We can listen with the intent to be supportive and build a bridge while being cautious to not become the ramp that merely slopes downward.

Energy vampires can wreak havoc on your energy distribution if you do not see them for who they are. Again, it feels amazing to be counted on and relied upon; it's one of the most refreshing and rewarding feelings I have ever felt. It is satisfying. An energy vampire is a person who drains the emotional, mental, or physical energy of others, often intentionally. They can be friends, family, colleagues, partners, or neighbors; relationships with them can be toxic. Energy vampires are more times than not, overly negative people who struggle with finding a positive aspect because they have adopted a dooming mindset that disrupts their ability to see things as opportunities and not inconveniences. Honestly speaking, if the energy you abide by includes Negative Nancies and Dooming Daniels, a beneficial, prosperous, and abundant reality is unlikely. Negative energy creates negative thoughts that translate into negative actions, ensuring plenty of negativity.

Other signs of energy vampires include those eager to gossip about others and belittle people to obtain or retain a feeling of superiority. At the end of the day, do you really want to be in the company of those who discuss people to hurt and not heal? We are known by the company we keep. Some characteristics of energy vampires include choosing to blame others over accountability, opting for complaining as opposed to changing, and favoring drama that gives them an opportunity to obtain the attention they seek by overexaggerating everything. Setting boundaries is the main way to rid yourself of energy vampires because their intolerance for change, especially when imposed by someone else, makes way for pushback and, in some instances, ghosting; the lack of accountability is insurmountable.

The Garbage Truck

People will find comfort in what we allow. For instance, if we allow a person to call us every day and unload the negative aspects of their day with little to no regard for our time are sanitation workers who have deemed us their personal dump. More often than not, people possibly mean well, but learned behavior will exist until change enters the chat; change is a challenge, so not many choose it. I am a recovering dump or a dumping survivor. While I have no regrets about establishing and introducing boundaries to relieve and sustain my mental health, I had to learn to revise the way I listened to others to protect myself. Despite my agenda being solely to lighten the load of a fellow human by "being there," the intention of another to dump the trash of their day on my doorstep, regularly, with no desire for resolution is an unconscionable, selfish act that warrants accountability and acknowledgment.

It is easier to teach a puppy than it is to train a dog. Once you hit your emotional reset button, we are introducing any innovative approaches necessary to either curtail the behaviors of others or to establish boundaries in new relationships, hence teaching or training. When it comes to instituting borders to protect our emotions from those who may trample upon them for their selfish satisfaction, the sooner, the better because it provides the clarity necessary to determine where you should invest your energy. By believing people to be who they are the first time, we allow our ears to hear what they say, and our eyes see the response of others. When we draw lines in the sand, we can better gauge where to invest our energy and who deserves our energy. To allow any person to address you in a manner that is not comfortable for you or is abusive, you create the foundation of a relationship possibly rooted in passive-aggressive exchanges that could either kill a perceived, budding relationship or cause the rotting of a relationship rooted in conflicting agendas and intentions once revealed.

The energy we consume has a transformative effect on our lives, which can lead to meaningful and lasting changes. Taking an approach that includes optimism, resilience, and a can-do attitude, we can successfully overcome obstacles that allow us to navigate challenges and achieve our goals with greater ease. Energy is contagious; when we radiate positivity, we attract like-minded individuals. We take the opportunity to uplift and support one another along our journeys of growth and development. There is the occurrence of a mindset shift that not only improves our well-being but also positively impacts those around us. When we lead by example and embody positive energy in our daily interactions and pursuits, we create a ripple effect that inspires others to embrace change, pursue their passions, and strive for personal excellence. By embracing positive energy, we can unlock limitless possibilities for self-improvement and transformation in every aspect of our lives.

I Eat First

Conceptually, I eat first is exactly what it sounds like: prioritizing yourself early and often in your life. It is taking care of yourself before you move forward with caring for anyone else, including children. This works for me because I was once a person who would go above and beyond for people, and I took pride in it; I was happy to help. I was so helpful that I would often table projects for myself to prioritize for others because they needed me, or so I thought. I was always ecstatic when people would call upon me for my assistance to utilize my talents because they needed me, even though they didn't. There came a time when I was taking stock in the middle of a substantial hardship. I had faith, but fear was attempting to rear its ugly head. I was in need, or so I thought, and for every hand I had been a help to, there was no hand extended to me; that was an eye-opener.

I am a firm believer that everything happens for a reason, and there is no such thing as coincidences so despite the inconvenience of the hardship, an opportunity was born. I learned in that very emotional, defeating moment that I must make a change, and that change would begin with me re-establishing my self-care, which would increase my self-confidence by strengthening my self-esteem to clear the path to self-actualization. My choice to change was one of the most difficult and necessary things I ever did because I had gotten so used to being the foreman that I forgot I was an architect. While I have enjoyed being "needed" in taking stock, I came to the realization that my helping hand, in many instances, had become the crutch that many had grown comfortable leaning upon; I was an enabler, now on the road to recovery and self-rediscovery.

With full knowledge, any change I made would impact the people who have grown accustomed to our relationships and the current workings. While it would be viewed as an inconvenience for some, it would give me an opportunity to gain insight and clarity into the basis and purpose of the relationship. In times of evaluation and observation, toxicity surfaces, if present, just as it is in administering tests, that weaknesses and strengths are revealed. I suspected that some relationships had run their course because, in my observations, it became clearer to me that in the one-sided relationships, I felt drained and depleted after any engagement; however, in other relationships, there were more supportive conversations that included encouraging language and provided an attentive listening ear. I made no attempt to impose my change upon others I simply began to modify the bad habits I had fostered to nourish the healthier mindset that welcomes the seeds of change to take root.

When prioritizing your energy and making changes in your life, it's important to ensure you eat first. Acknowledge the things that drain your energy and make a conscious effort to actively remove them from your daily routine one day at a time. Habits are routines developed over time, and the patience that we allot ourselves amid changes fuels our perseverance and resilience toward consistency. When we begin setting boundaries with people who constantly demand our time and attention or take stock of relationships that no longer align with our long-term goals, we lose them because while intentions were admirable, their agendas were deceitful. We must conserve our energy for things that bring joy and fulfillment to provide beneficial motivation and drive toward positive changes in our lives. Because it's okay to say no to things that don't serve you well, it's important to listen to your instincts when deciding where to invest your time and energy. Trust yourself and prioritize self-care to make meaningful changes with clarity and purpose.

Energy and change are essential parts of our everyday lives. When we feel like our growth is stifled, stuck in a rut, or uninspired, change would be a welcome seed fit to be planted in the disrupted, agitated soil. By trying something new or stepping out of our comfort zone, we ignite a spark of creativity and bring about positive change. The energy surrounding us propels us forward and drives us to embrace change. Embarking upon change can be daunting at first, but once harnessed, we can use the energy cultivated by the change to propel ourselves toward growth and new experiences, laying the path to the best versions of ourselves.

Consistency and self-awareness are key to maintaining changes. When prioritizing a positive mindset and being more selective about your energy, you are doing the necessary groundwork to grease the wheels toward success. It's not just about making a change or adopting a positive outlook; it's about actively choosing to stick with it every day. Whether through practicing gratitude, setting realistic goals, or surrounding yourself with uplifting people, the key is to make these habits a part of your routine. Reward yourself for your progress because staying positive can help you push through those tough times. Stay committed to your growth, and remember that little by little, day by day, you're making strides toward a happier and healthier you.

My Personal Quotes...little gems that got me going and keep me going...

- Stop investing in people who don't invest in you; it's like making deposits in an account where you can't withdraw.

- You can't pour into others if you're empty; self-care is imperative, important, and immediate.

- The hardest lessons to learn have the most tests.

- Be careful when looking for yourself in others, it's like following a stranger home.

- Don't be so distracted by what happened that you miss what's happening.

- Do not miss the message because you're focused on the messenger.

- God is my accountant because I had a habit of spending too much time, paying people too much attention.

- Change is a pain that is self-inflicted.

- Change changes you, so stop going where you

used to go when you're not who you used to be.

- Be the reason it happened or the reason it's happening.
- We are spiritual beings having a human experience, which means we should not be humans being; we should be humans doing.
- Patience is important during your pursuit of peace, and peace of mind is paramount.
- Learning to listen with your eyes and ears is an acquired skill, learn it.
- Pain is the oil that gets you to the wheels of change and consistency is the vessel that keeps it going.
- The absence of my presence is the absence of my presents because my presence is a gift.
- God does my gardening because He sees gardens where I do not have roots but some seeds.
- You must give people room to do what they want to do so you can see what they'd rather do.
- Actions are most honest when no one's paying attention.

- Being alone is a choice of the mind, feeling lonely is a deception of your thoughts.
- Accountability is the opportunity you give yourself to no longer be triggered.
- When you own your shit, it cannot be used by someone else as ammunition.
- The more time we put into building our character, the less time we have to put into repairs.
- How will you ever get what is for you when you are standing in the shadows of someone else's shine?
- If you choose to be parallel and ordinary, you will never know how extraordinary you can be.
- Being complacent stifles your growth. It is the equivalent of chaining yourself to a bolder and choosing to walk in place for the rest of your life.
- You cannot live inside your mind; you're not alone.
- It is when you are alone that you get to know yourself best.
- Take comfort in letting go because what is to

come will be far greater.

- Decide you want peace and choose silence as the vessel.
- Procrastination has killed more dreams than comfort.
- If someone doesn't appreciate your presence, bless them with your absence.
- Never let someone else's opinion of you become your reality.
- If you own your flaws, they can't be weaponized against you to make you feel bad or bring you down.
- Anger is the punishment you give yourself when you allow someone else's words to change your emotions or feelings.
- You have the right to remain silent.
- Change starts with your mind, and that's where the seeds of success are sown.
- Life's lessons and blessings are the building blocks that create the many versions of ourselves that appear in the different chapters of our lives.

THE WAIT OF CHANGE:
TRUSTING THE PROCESS

WORKBOOK
AND JOURNAL

LET'S UNDERTAKE A MIND EXPANDING, REALITY ALTERING
JOURNEY THAT WILL LEAVE YOU EMPOWERED AND READY
TO CONQUER FEAR AND OVERCOME LIMITING BELIEFS

Table of contents

RATE YOUR
THINKING

LOOK AT THE LIFE AREAS BELOW AND RATE YOURSELF BETWEEN 1-10
WITH HOW SELF-AWARE AND CONFIDENT YOU ARE IN EACH CATEGORY.

BELIEF IN YOURSELF

| 1 | 2 | 3 | 4 | 5 | 6 | 7 | 8 | 9 | 10 |

NOT VERY   EXTREMELY

ABILITY TO BE POSITIVE

| 1 | 2 | 3 | 4 | 5 | 6 | 7 | 8 | 9 | 10 |

NOT VERY   EXTREMELY

FLEXIBLE ATTITUDE

| 1 | 2 | 3 | 4 | 5 | 6 | 7 | 8 | 9 | 10 |

NOT VERY   EXTREMELY

DECISION MAKING

| 1 | 2 | 3 | 4 | 5 | 6 | 7 | 8 | 9 | 10 |

NOT VERY   EXTREMELY

ABILITY TO STICK TO GOALS

| 1 | 2 | 3 | 4 | 5 | 6 | 7 | 8 | 9 | 10 |

NOT VERY   EXTREMELY

01 Introduction

Confucius says, "To put the world in order, we must first put the nation in order; to put the nation in order, we must first put the family in order; to put the family in order; we must first cultivate our personal life; we must first set out hearts right."

Confucius' quote is intriguing in the sense that simplistically, he was advising that to evoke change, we must change as we are the source of the need for change. Despite the quote being dated, its relevance in society today is substantial.

Would it shock you to know that studies show that comfort kills more dreams than procrastination? If those studies are true that would mean the same comfort we spent a lifetime pursuing is the same thief that robs us of our drive, passion, and determination to conquer, succeed, or grow. Change is an inevitable certainty. Without change, there is no growth. Without growth we are left with a stagnated society with constant remakes or duplicates of copies.

02 Welcome

Welcome to this empowering journey! This workbook is designed with a clear purpose - to guide you towards a more fulfilling and meaningful life. Your commitment to this personal transformation process is the key to unlocking a path of self-discovery and positive change.

Remember, this is your journey, and the commitment you make today is a powerful step towards living a life that reflects your true desires and potential. Let's begin this transformative process together!

03   What Is Change?

Change is choosing to abandon comfort for the reality you deserve. By choosing to change, the next step is to change your mindset. Changing how our brain has functioned for years, is not an easy task but we must be pushed by the pain of operating in an old mindset until we are pulled to make the change. We must set our minds for the process of change. A changed mind leads to changed thoughts, actions, and reality. We must grant change the space to exist within us, expand into the environment around us, and evoke it when the opportunity presents itself. Change is a phenomenal thing that allows for the fulfillment of our expectations. Change is a vessel that will enable us to envision possibilities as we demolish obstacles, self-imposed and otherwise. Change is every opportunity that we encounter daily. Take a chance on change.

04 Faith

Faith is traditionally tied to a higher power. The energy or power greater than yourself provides guidance and orders the steps of our plan. In instances where you experience missteps or you've lost your footing on the path, any confusion you feel is a distraction. Take a couple of breaths, allow your mind to reset, and move on; that is not a divine distraction. Even if you have gotten off the path, the last thing you want to do is to take time to engage in something negative like beating yourself up, nope, that would be the true distraction. Setting goals, and introducing as many steps as YOU need is a great way to stay on track with the desire to change.

1. Personal Goals:
   - What milestones do you want to achieve in your personal life?
   - What would make your life more fulfilling?
2. Professional Goals:
   - What are your ambitions and achievements in your career?
   - How do you envision yourself professionally in one or five years?

TRUST

the

PROCESS

05 Surrender..Letting Go

By choosing change we must surrender our old ways. Essentially by choosing to change or deciding that the path we are traveling no longer makes sense or we've decided to walk in our purpose, letting go of people, places, and things that no longer serve us and will be of no use in the next chapter of our life. Because we get comfortable in different chapters of our lives, we tend to "linger" in circumstances and situations we have outgrown. Letting go isn't easy but it's imperative to change and the success of the process. Get out of the way of change, you made the choice.

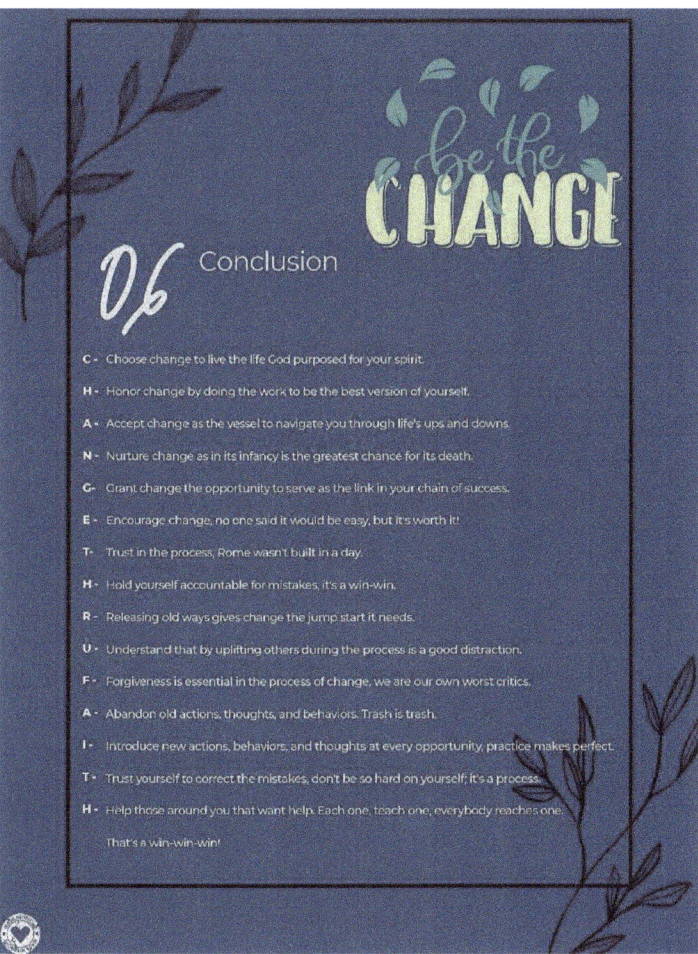

06 Conclusion

be the CHANGE

C - Choose change to live the life God purposed for your spirit.

H - Honor change by doing the work to be the best version of yourself.

A - Accept change as the vessel to navigate you through life's ups and downs.

N - Nurture change as in its infancy is the greatest chance for its death.

G - Grant change the opportunity to serve as the link in your chain of success.

E - Encourage change, no one said it would be easy, but it's worth it!

T - Trust in the process, Rome wasn't built in a day.

H - Hold yourself accountable for mistakes, it's a win-win.

R - Releasing old ways gives change the jump start it needs.

U - Understand that by uplifting others during the process is a good distraction.

F - Forgiveness is essential in the process of change, we are our own worst critics.

A - Abandon old actions, thoughts, and behaviors. Trash is trash.

I - Introduce new actions, behaviors, and thoughts at every opportunity, practice makes perfect.

T - Trust yourself to correct the mistakes, don't be so hard on yourself; it's a process.

H - Help those around you that want help. Each one, teach one, everybody reaches one.

That's a win-win-win!

SELF-CARE PLANNER

Date:

Goals for my mind

Goals for my body

Note to self

Reminder

MORNING MANTRA

I am capable, strong, and ready to take on the day.

_____

Today, I choose joy, peace, and positivity in all I do.

_____

I radiate confidence, love, and kindness in all interactions.

_____

I am in control of my thoughts, emotions, and actions today.

_____

I have everything I need to succeed within me.

_____

I welcome positivity into my life today and always.

_____

My mind is clear, my heart is open, and I am ready to embrace the day.

_____

I am resilient, and I embrace challenges as opportunities for growth.

Choose or create a mantra that resonates deeply with you and reflects the mindset or attitude you wish to embody throughout your day. Repeat it to yourself as part of your morning routine, perhaps during meditation, while getting ready, or whenever it feels most effective for you. This repetition can help focus your mind and set a positive intention for the day ahead.

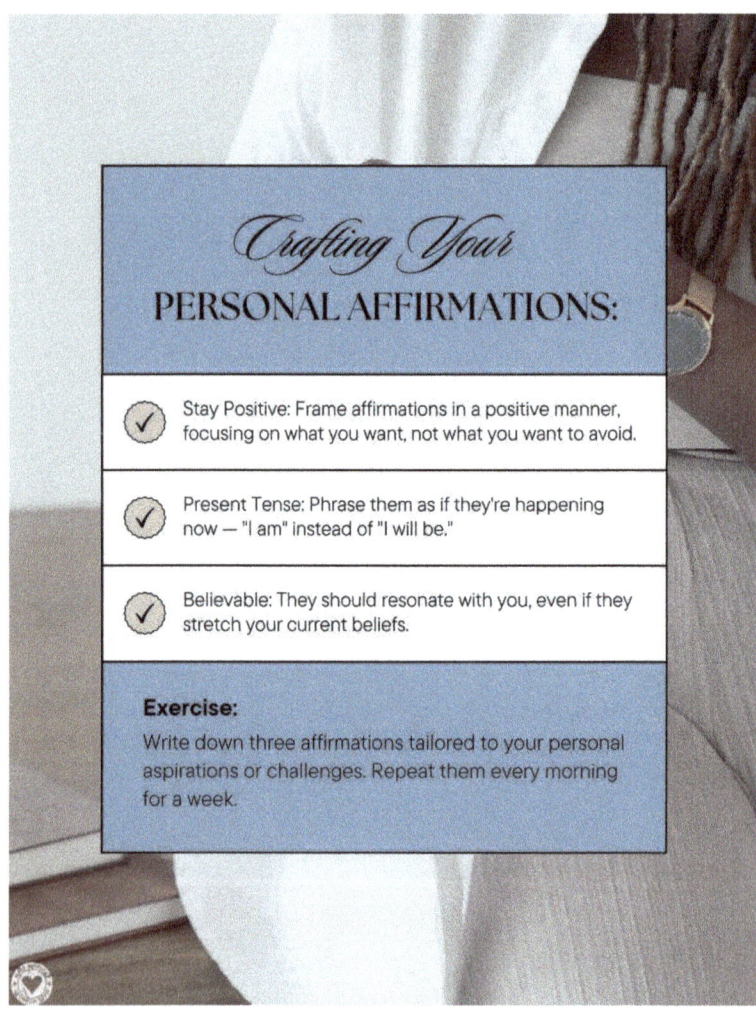

Crafting Your
PERSONAL AFFIRMATIONS:

✓ Stay Positive: Frame affirmations in a positive manner, focusing on what you want, not what you want to avoid.

✓ Present Tense: Phrase them as if they're happening now — "I am" instead of "I will be."

✓ Believable: They should resonate with you, even if they stretch your current beliefs.

Exercise:
Write down three affirmations tailored to your personal aspirations or challenges. Repeat them every morning for a week.

28-DAY GRATITUDE JOURNAL CHALLENGE

DAY	WEEK 1	WEEK 2	WEEK 3	WEEK 4
1	Write down three things you are grateful for today.	Call or text someone you appreciate and let them know why you are grateful for them.	Write about a person who has positively impacted your life and why you are thankful for them.	Make a list of five things that bring you joy and gratitude.
2	Take a moment to appreciate something in nature, whether it be a beautiful view or the feeling of the sun on your skin.	Write about a place you are grateful for, whether it be your home, a favorite vacation spot, or a cozy coffee shop.	Think about a talent or skill you have that you are grateful for and write about how it has positively impacted your life.	Write a thank you note to someone who has made a difference in your life.
3	Write about a moment or experience that made you feel grateful or blessed.	Take a moment to appreciate your body and write about three things you are thankful for in regards to your health.	Write about a material possession you are grateful for and why it brings you joy.	Take a moment to appreciate your job or career and write about how it has positively impacted your life.
4	Write about a friend or family member who has been there for you through thick and thin, and how they have positively impacted your life.	Make a list of five things you are looking forward to in the future and why you are grateful for them.	Take a moment to appreciate your community and write about something you are thankful for in regards to where you live.	Write about a book or movie that has inspired you and how you are grateful for its impact on your life.
5	Write about a time when someone showed you kindness and how it impacted your life.	Write about a spiritual belief or practice that brings you gratitude and peace.	Take a moment to appreciate the technology you use on a daily basis and write about how it has positively impacted your life.	Write about a food or meal you are grateful for and why it brings you joy.
6	Write about a challenge or obstacle that you are grateful for because it taught you something important.	Make a list of ten things you are grateful for right now.	Write about a pet or animal you are grateful for and how they bring joy to your life.	Take a moment to appreciate your senses (sight, smell, taste, touch, and hearing) and write about three things you are grateful for in regards to each sense.
7	Write about a teacher or mentor who has positively impacted your life and how you are grateful for their influence.	Take a moment to appreciate your sense of humor and write about three things that make you laugh or smile.	Write about a historical figure or event that you are grateful for and how it has positively impacted your life.	Make a list of three things you are grateful for in regards to your personal growth or development.

133

Weekly Meeting

Week 1

Week 2

Week 3

Week 4

Notes:

Weekly Meeting

Week 1

Week 2

Week 3

Week 4

Notes:

Weekly Meeting

Week 1

Week 2

Week 3

Week 4

Notes:

Weekly Meeting

Week 1

Week 2

Week 3

Week 4

Notes:

MONTHLY PLANNER

MONTH OF

My Focus is on	My Vision is

I'm Excited for	I'm Grateful for
To-do	Main Goals
☐	#1
☐	#2
☐	#3
☐	#4
☐	#5

☐	#6
☐	#7
☐	#8

APPOINTMENTS & DEADLINES BIRTHDAYS

Date:

BRAIN DUMP

Date:

BRAIN DUMP

Date:

BRAIN DUMP

Date:

BRAIN DUMP

About The Author

Katrina E. Johnson is an ordained minister and spiritual life coach with a strong desire to enlighten and encourage the collective to embark upon a journey of spiritual growth and self-rediscovery. She aims to serve as a light to anyone and everyone who has cast out fear and chosen change despite its challenges. With change, we are Choosing How Accountability Navigates Good Energy. Remember: Today is a good day to...